FOUR-FISTED
TALES

ANIMALS
IN COMBAT

BEN TOWLE

DEAD
RECKONING
ANNAPOLIS, MARYLAND

Published by Dead Reckoning
291 Wood Road
Annapolis, MD 21402

Library of Congress Cataloging-in-Publication Data
Names: Towle, Ben, author, illustrator.
Title: Four-fisted tales : animals in combat / Ben Towle.
Description: Annapolis, Maryland : Dead Reckoning, [2021]
Identifiers: LCCN 2021005680 (print) | LCCN 2021005681 (ebook) | ISBN 9781682474167
   (paperback) | ISBN 9781682477038 (epub) | ISBN 9781682477038 (pdf)
Subjects: LCSH: Animals—War use—Comic books, strips, etc. | Animals—Biography—
   Comic books, strips, etc. | Human-animal relationships—Comic books, strips, etc.
Classification: LCC UH87 .T69 2021 (print) | LCC UH87 (ebook) | DDC 355.4/24—dc23
LC record available at https://lccn.loc.gov/2021005680
LC ebook record available at https://lccn.loc.gov/2021005681

♾ Print editions meet the requirements of ANSI/NISO z39.48-1992 (Permanence of Paper).
Printed in the United States of America.

29 28 27 26 25 24 23 22 21   9 8 7 6 5 4 3 2 1
First printing

FOUR-FISTED TALES was drawn in Clip Studio Paint
and digitally hand lettered over the Blambot typefaces
Mighty Zeo 2.0 and Jack Armstrong. Sound effects
lettering was hand drawn with the utmost admiration
for the great Ben Oda.

"They had no choice."

--Inscription, Animals in War Memorial, London

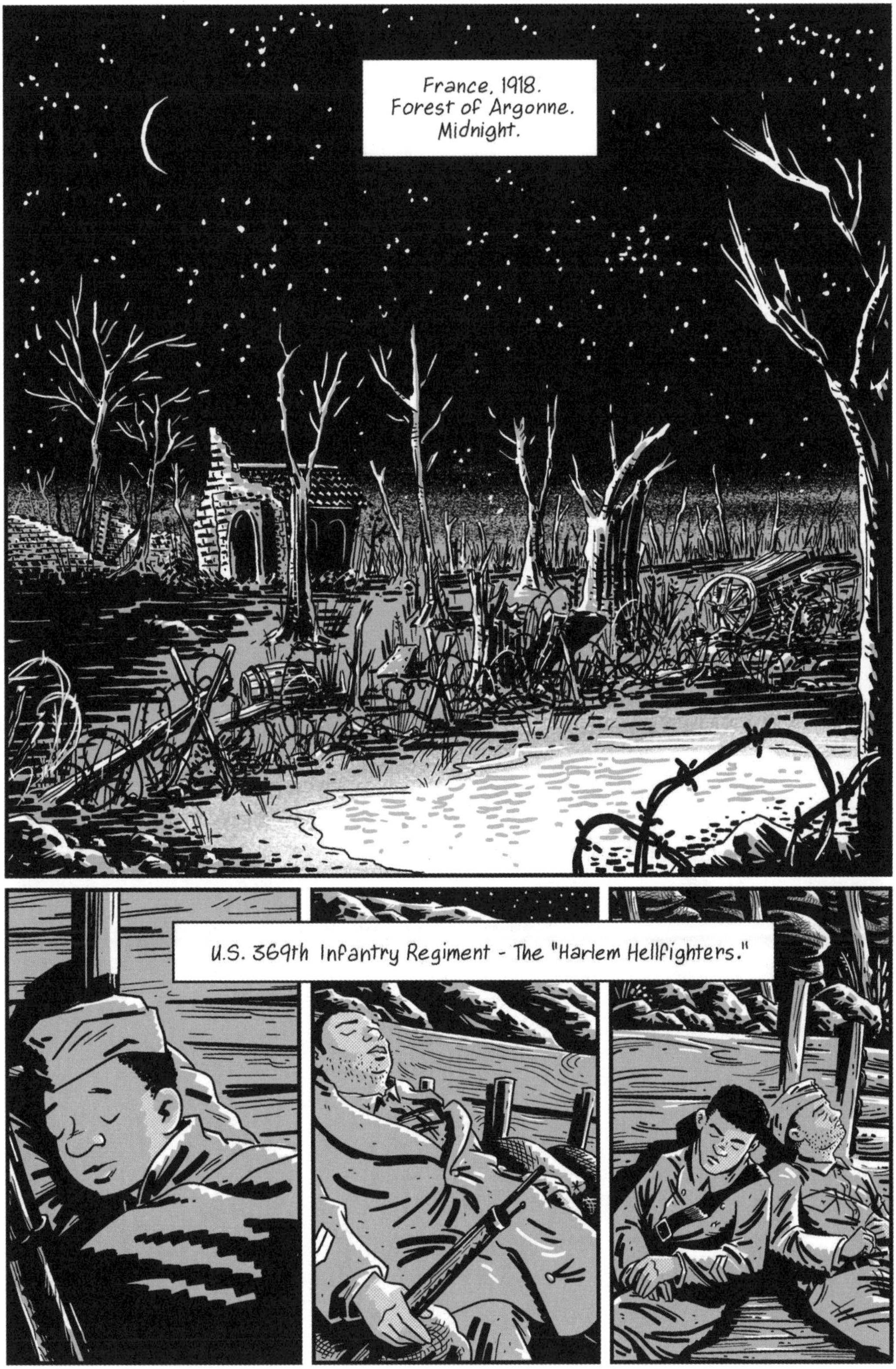
France, 1918.
Forest of Argonne.
Midnight.
U.S. 369th Infantry Regiment - The "Harlem Hellfighters."

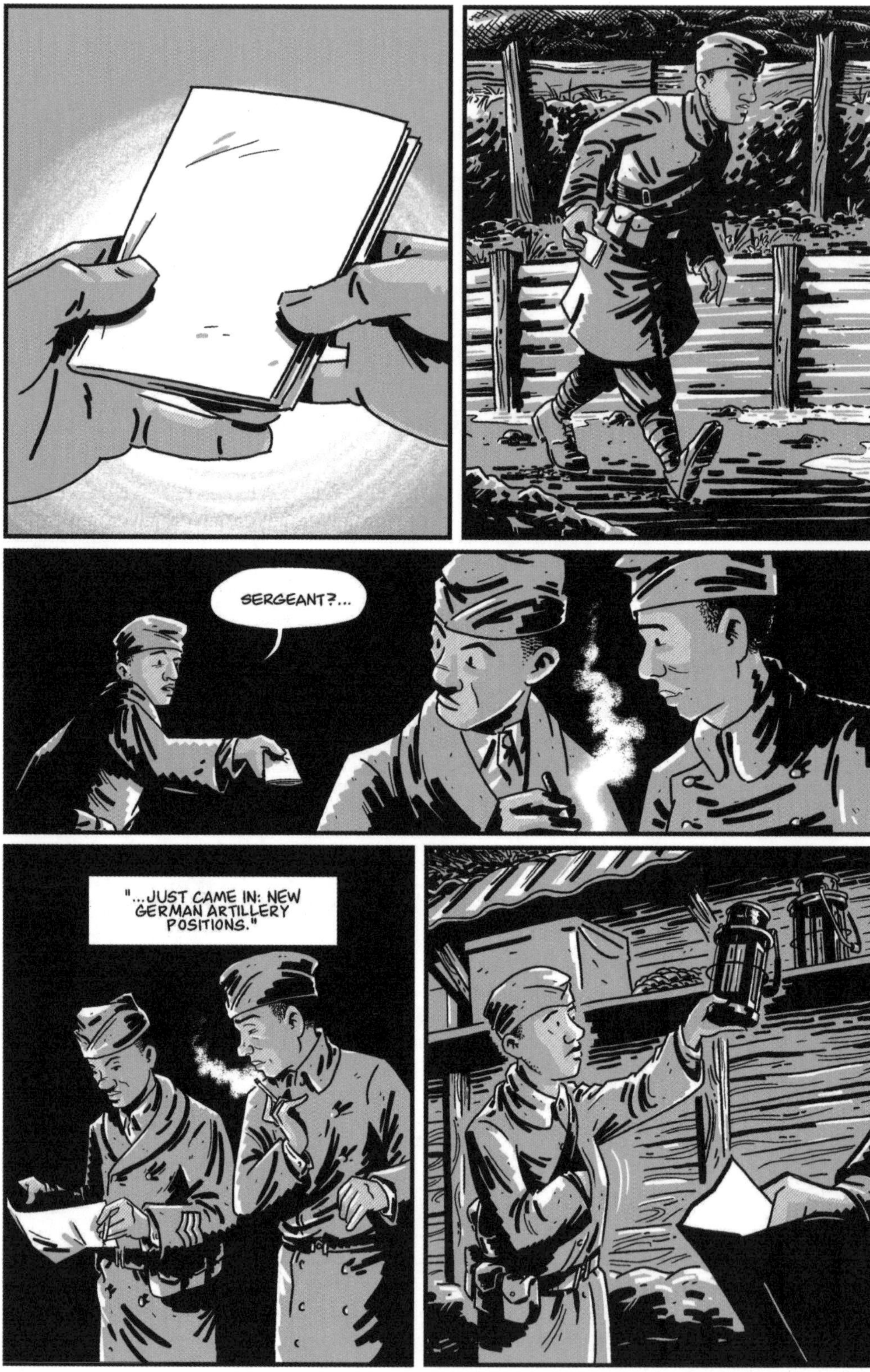
SERGEANT?...
"...JUST CAME IN: NEW GERMAN ARTILLERY POSITIONS."

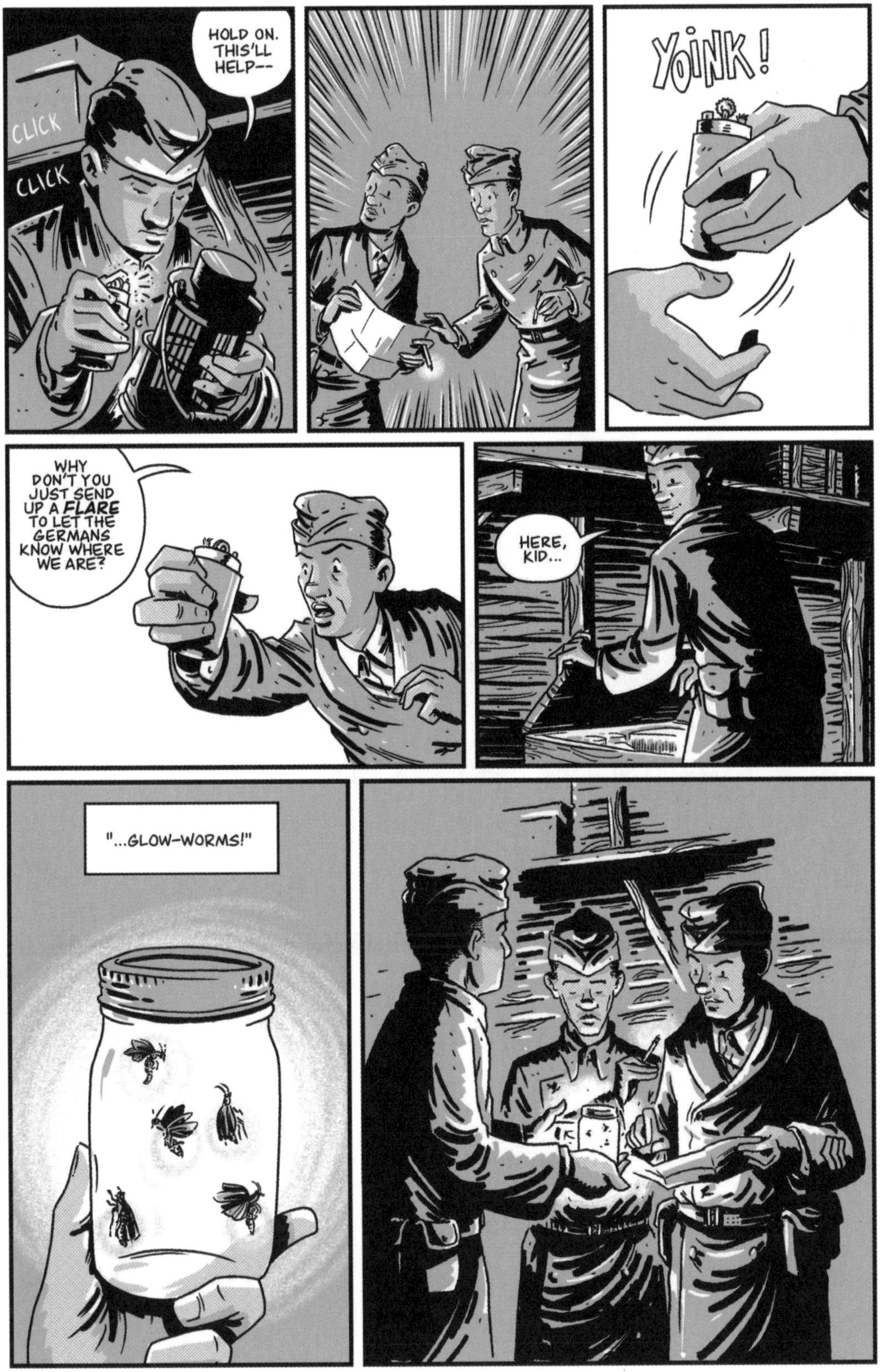

HOLD ON. THIS'LL HELP--
CLICK
CLICK
YOINK!
WHY DON'T YOU JUST SEND UP A FLARE TO LET THE GERMANS KNOW WHERE WE ARE?
HERE, KID...
"...GLOW-WORMS!"

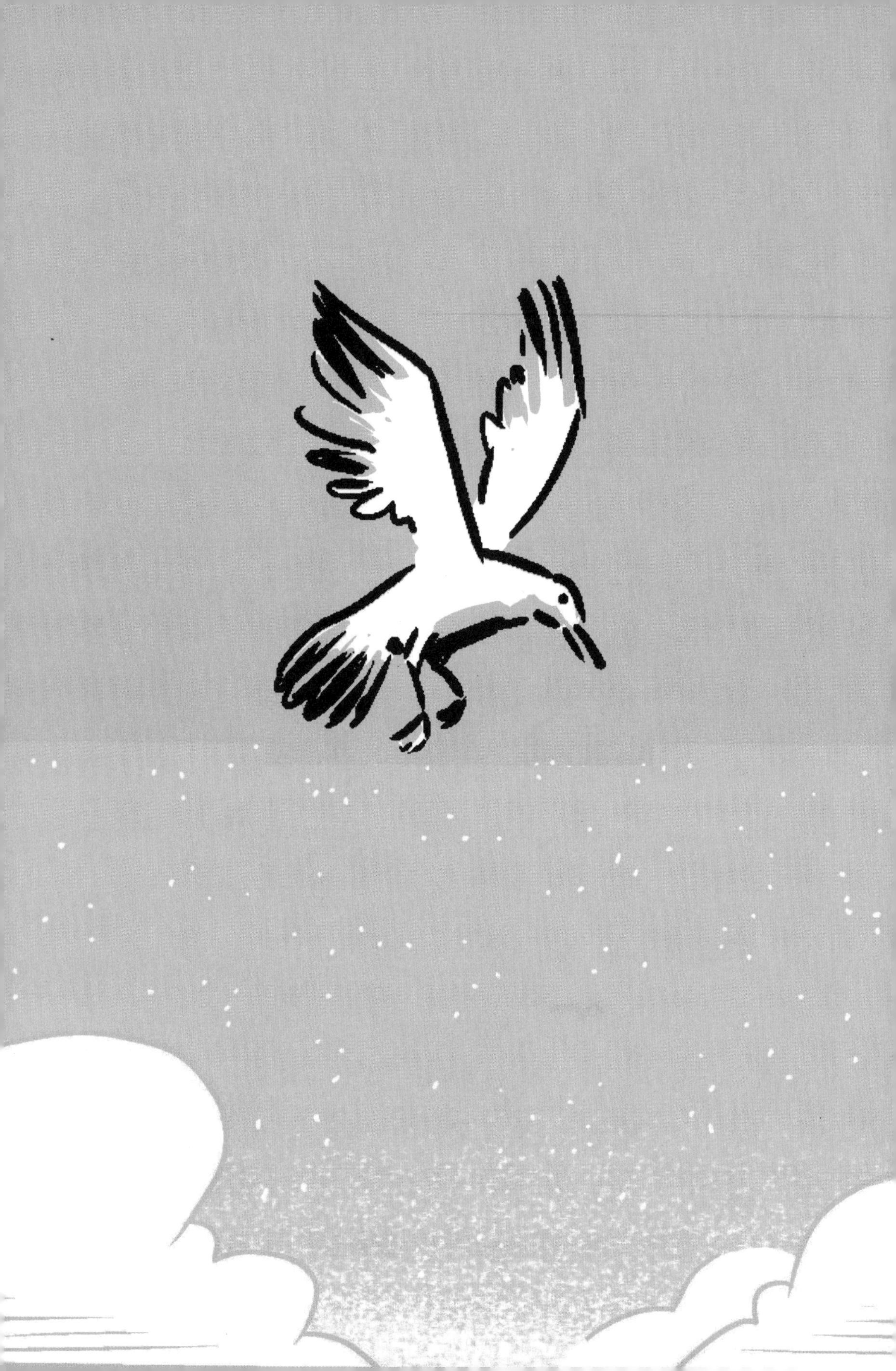

CONTENTS

JACK

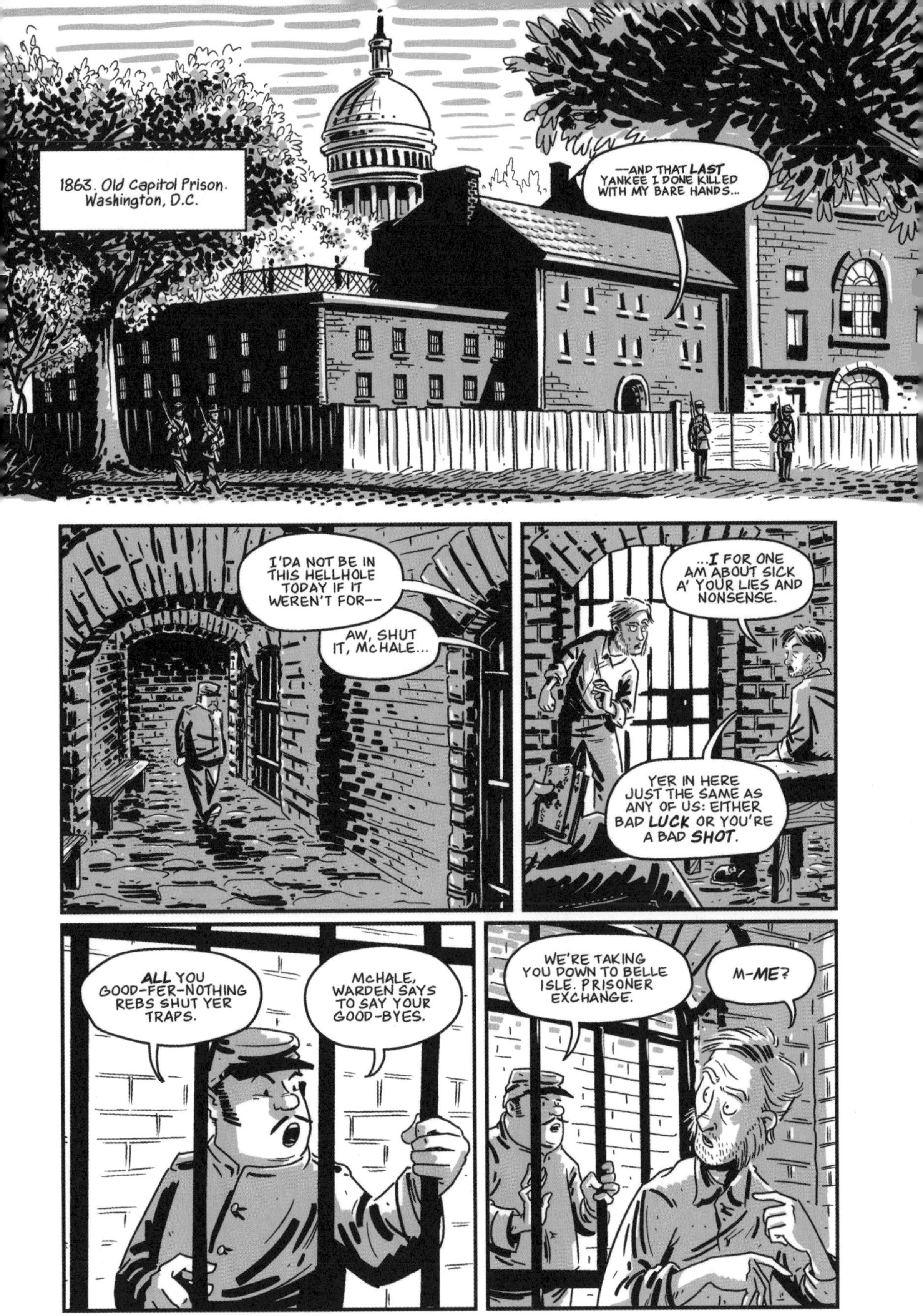
1863. Old Capitol Prison. Washington, D.C.
--AND THAT LAST YANKEE I DONE KILLED WITH MY BARE HANDS...
I'DA NOT BE IN THIS HELLHOLE TODAY IF IT WEREN'T FOR--
AW, SHUT IT, McHALE...
...I FOR ONE AM ABOUT SICK A' YOUR LIES AND NONSENSE.
YER IN HERE JUST THE SAME AS ANY OF US: EITHER BAD LUCK OR YOU'RE A BAD SHOT.
ALL YOU GOOD-FER-NOTHING REBS SHUT YER TRAPS.
McHALE, WARDEN SAYS TO SAY YOUR GOOD-BYES.
WE'RE TAKING YOU DOWN TO BELLE ISLE. PRISONER EXCHANGE.
M-ME?

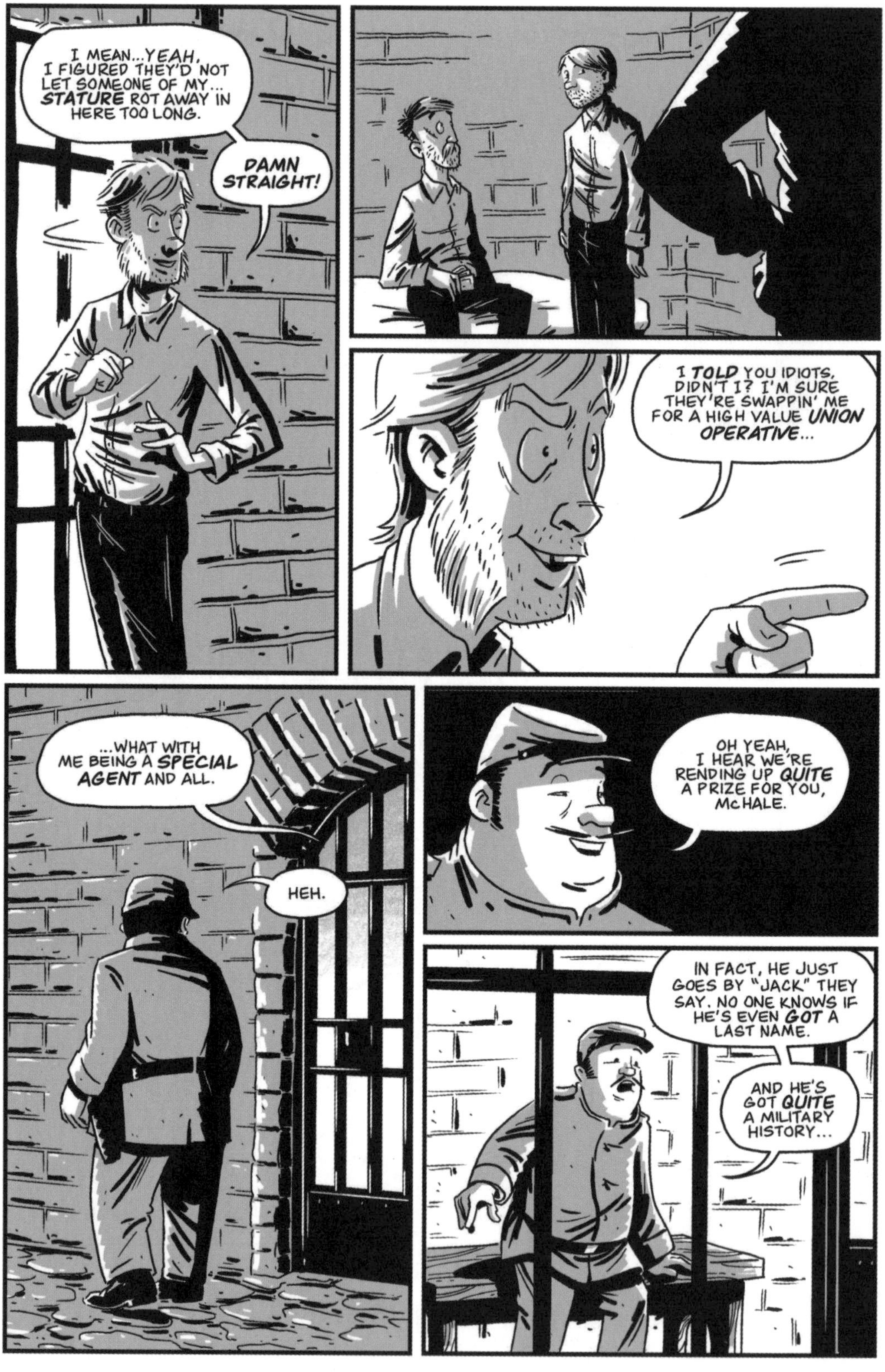
I MEAN...YEAH, I FIGURED THEY'D NOT LET SOMEONE OF MY... STATURE ROT AWAY IN HERE TOO LONG.
DAMN STRAIGHT!
I TOLD YOU IDIOTS, DIDN'T I? I'M SURE THEY'RE SWAPPIN' ME FOR A HIGH VALUE UNION OPERATIVE...
...WHAT WITH ME BEING A SPECIAL AGENT AND ALL.
HEH.
OH YEAH, I HEAR WE'RE RENDING UP QUITE A PRIZE FOR YOU, McHALE.
IN FACT, HE JUST GOES BY "JACK" THEY SAY. NO ONE KNOWS IF HE'S EVEN GOT A LAST NAME.
AND HE'S GOT QUITE A MILITARY HISTORY...

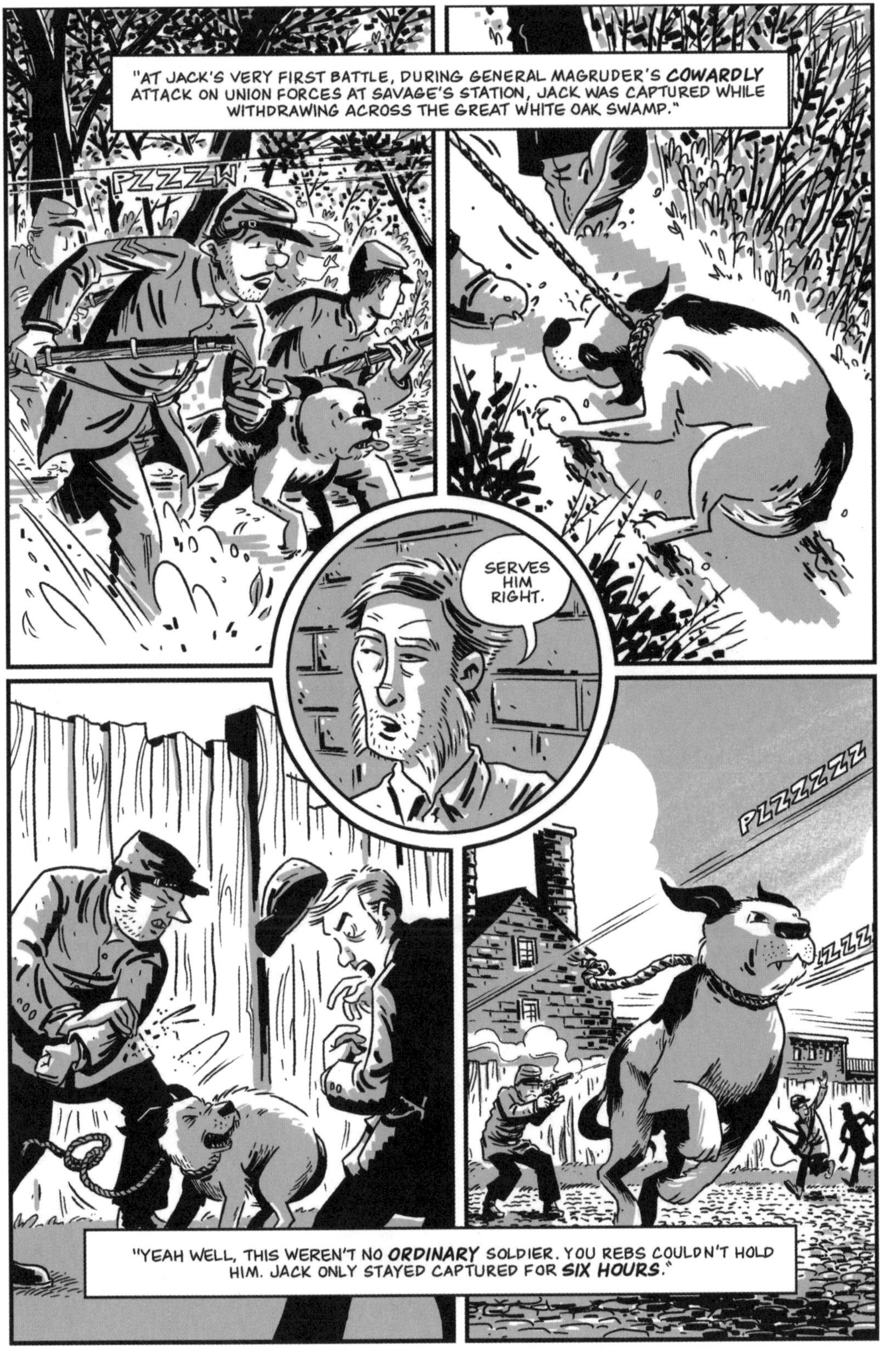
"AT JACK'S VERY FIRST BATTLE, DURING GENERAL MAGRUDER'S COWARDLY ATTACK ON UNION FORCES AT SAVAGE'S STATION, JACK WAS CAPTURED WHILE WITHDRAWING ACROSS THE GREAT WHITE OAK SWAMP."
PZZZW
SERVES HIM RIGHT.
PLZZZZZZ
ZZZZ
"YEAH WELL, THIS WEREN'T NO ORDINARY SOLDIER. YOU REBS COULDN'T HOLD HIM. JACK ONLY STAYED CAPTURED FOR SIX HOURS."

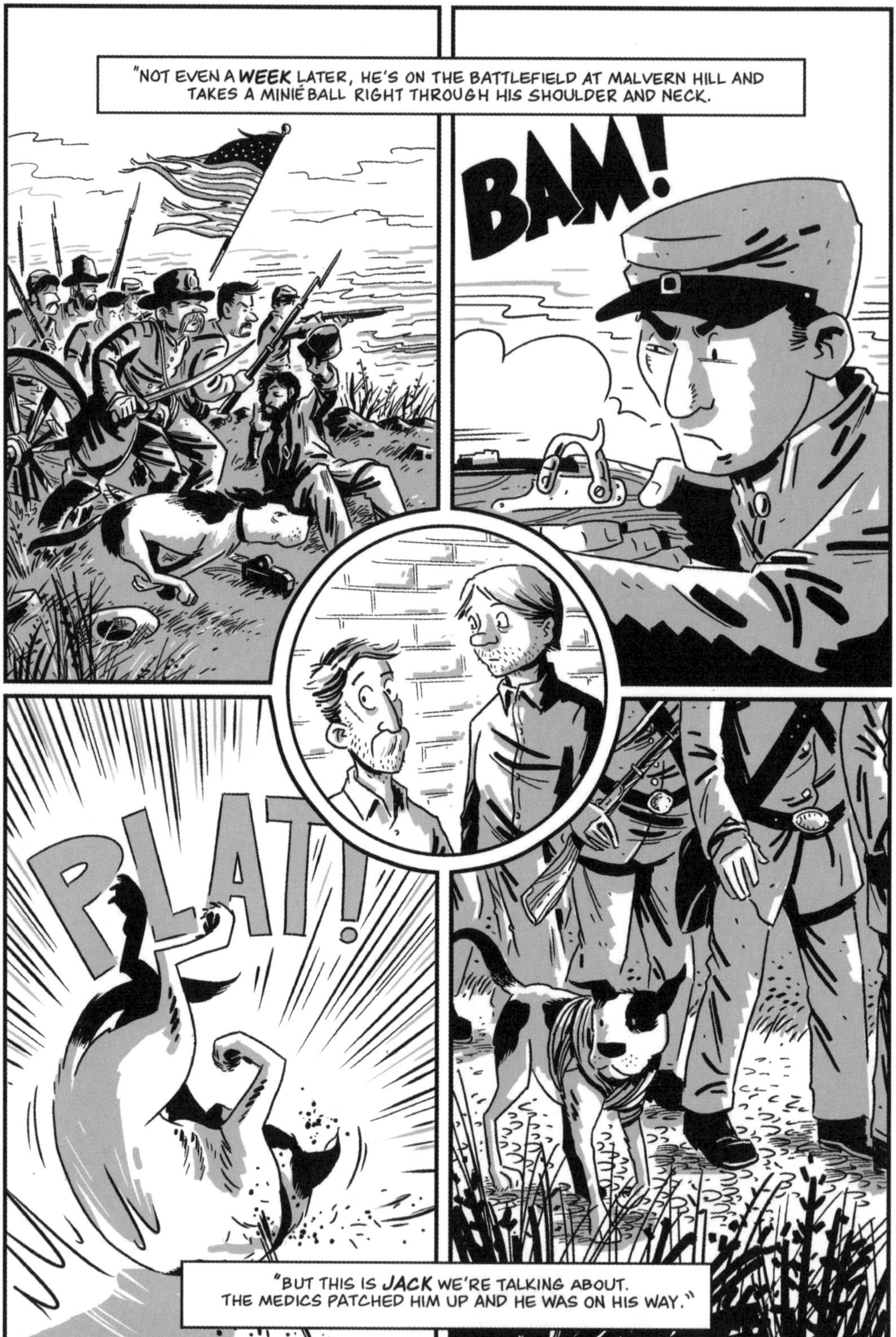
"NOT EVEN A WEEK LATER, HE'S ON THE BATTLEFIELD AT MALVERN HILL AND TAKES A MINIÉ BALL RIGHT THROUGH HIS SHOULDER AND NECK.
BAM!
PLAT!
"BUT THIS IS JACK WE'RE TALKING ABOUT. THE MEDICS PATCHED HIM UP AND HE WAS ON HIS WAY."

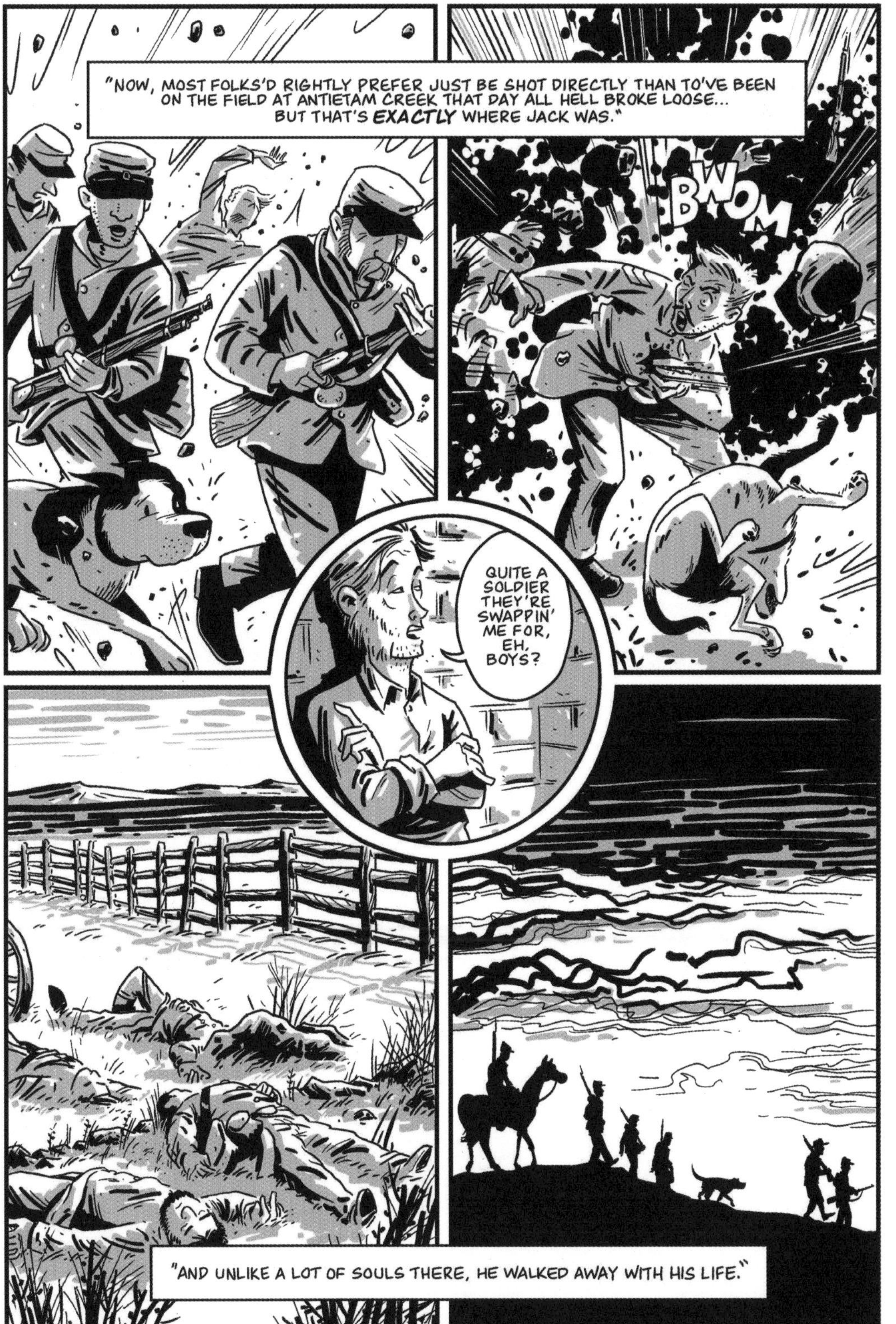
"NOW, MOST FOLKS'D RIGHTLY PREFER JUST BE SHOT DIRECTLY THAN TO'VE BEEN ON THE FIELD AT ANTIETAM CREEK THAT DAY ALL HELL BROKE LOOSE... BUT THAT'S EXACTLY WHERE JACK WAS."
BWOM
QUITE A SOLDIER THEY'RE SWAPPIN' ME FOR, EH, BOYS?
"AND UNLIKE A LOT OF SOULS THERE, HE WALKED AWAY WITH HIS LIFE."

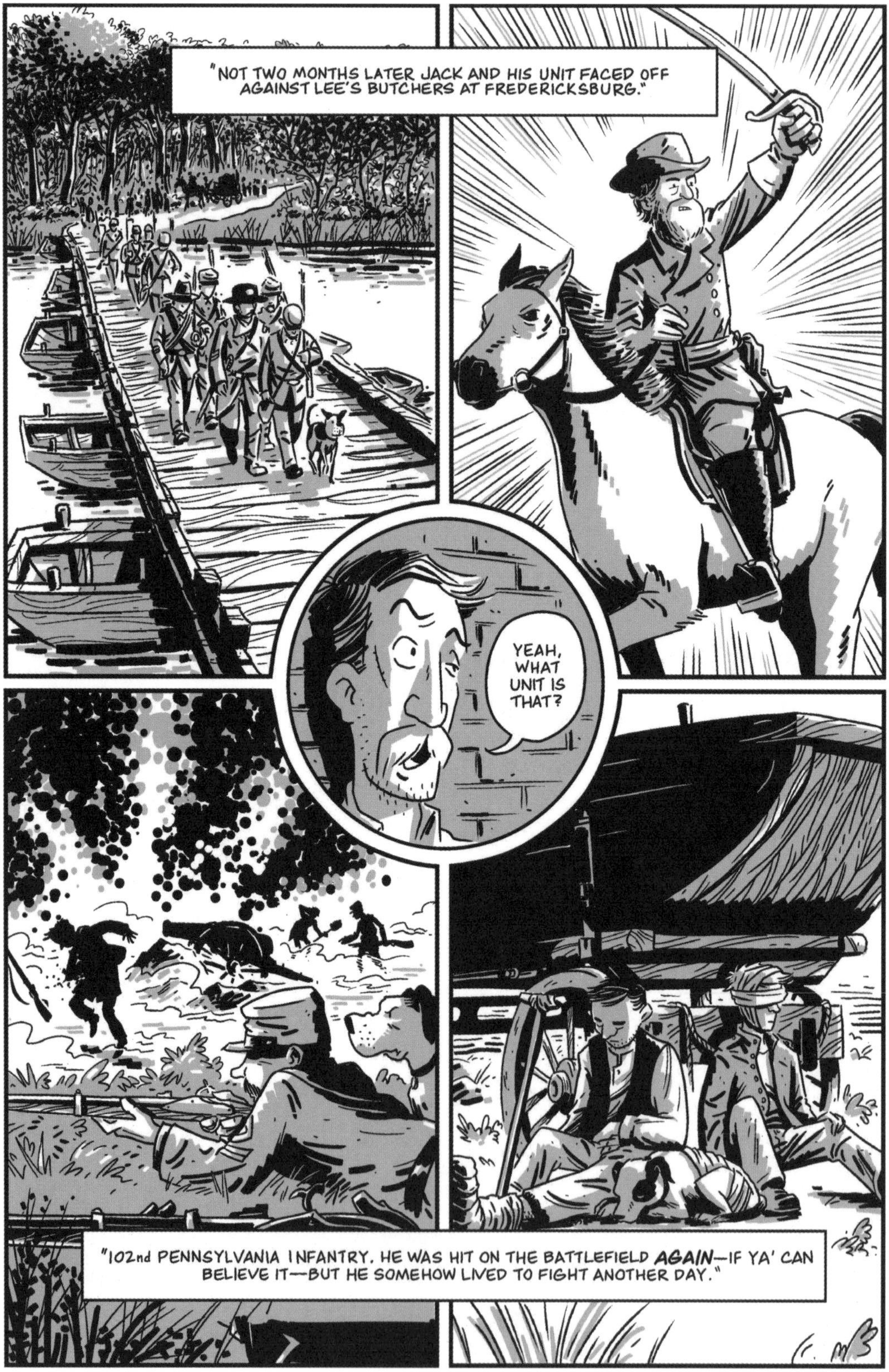
"NOT TWO MONTHS LATER JACK AND HIS UNIT FACED OFF AGAINST LEE'S BUTCHERS AT FREDERICKSBURG."
YEAH, WHAT UNIT IS THAT?
"102nd PENNSYLVANIA INFANTRY. HE WAS HIT ON THE BATTLEFIELD AGAIN—IF YA' CAN BELIEVE IT—BUT HE SOMEHOW LIVED TO FIGHT ANOTHER DAY."

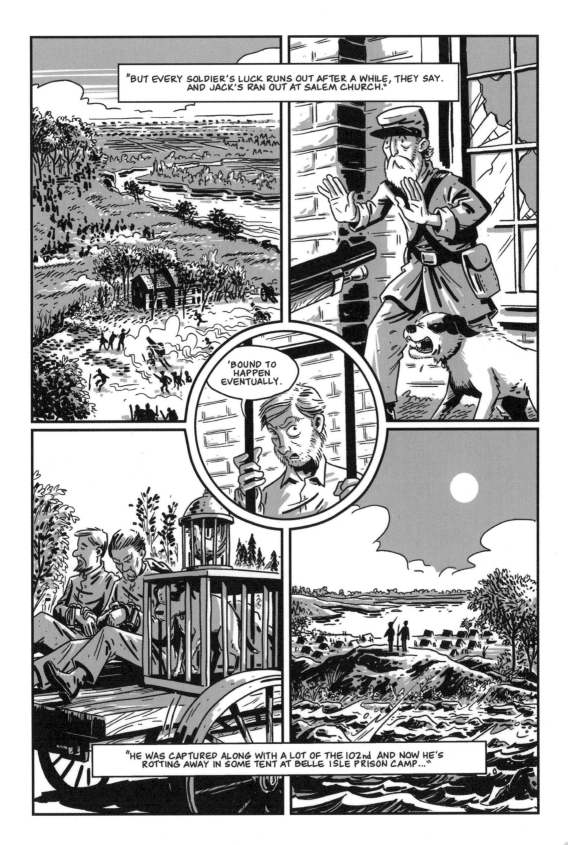

"BUT EVERY SOLDIER'S LUCK RUNS OUT AFTER A WHILE, THEY SAY. AND JACK'S RAN OUT AT SALEM CHURCH."

'BOUND TO HAPPEN EVENTUALLY.

"HE WAS CAPTURED ALONG WITH A LOT OF THE 102nd AND NOW HE'S ROTTING AWAY IN SOME TENT AT BELLE ISLE PRISON CAMP..."

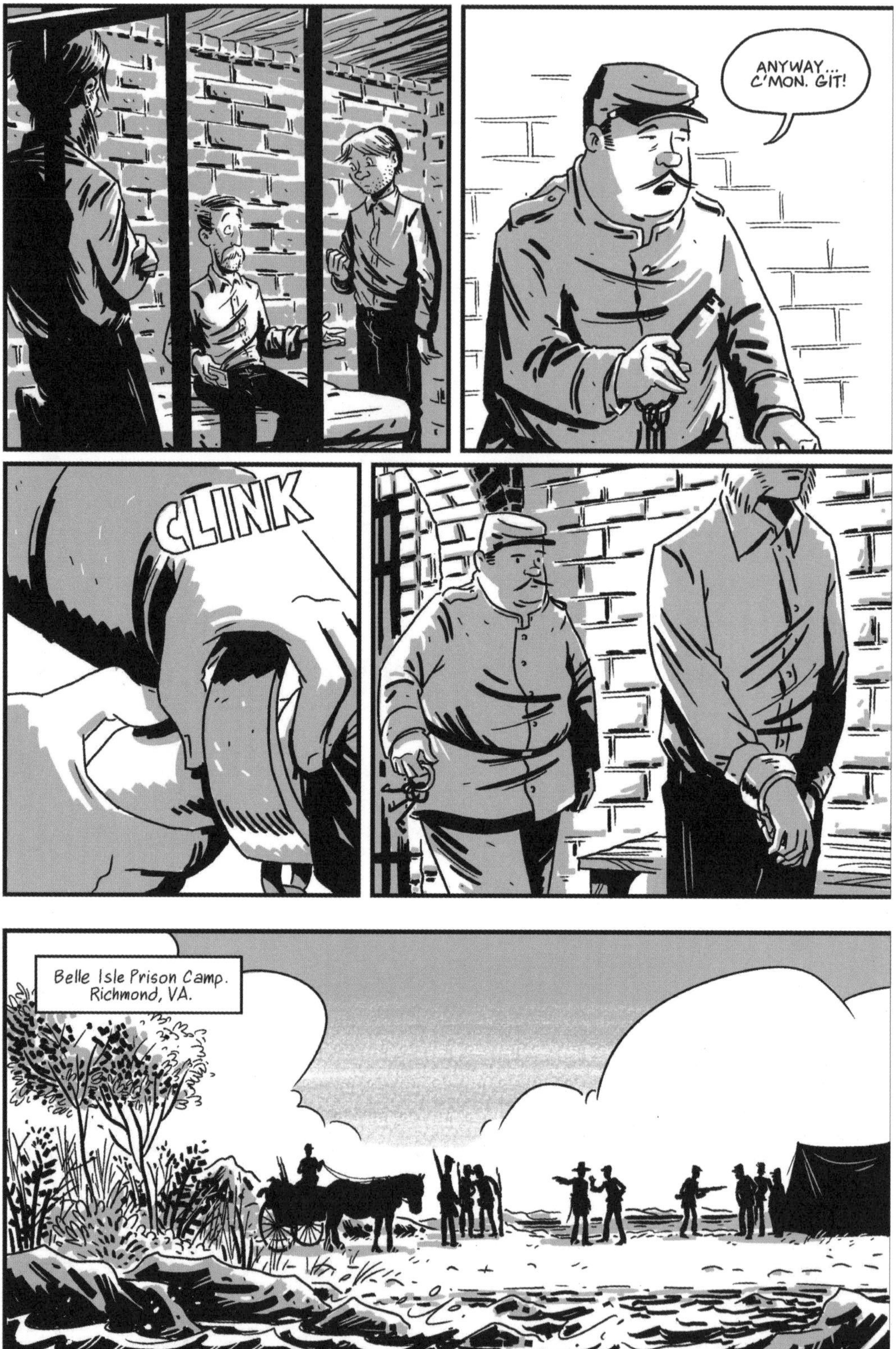
ANYWAY... C'MON. GIT!
CLINK
Belle Isle Prison Camp. Richmond, VA.

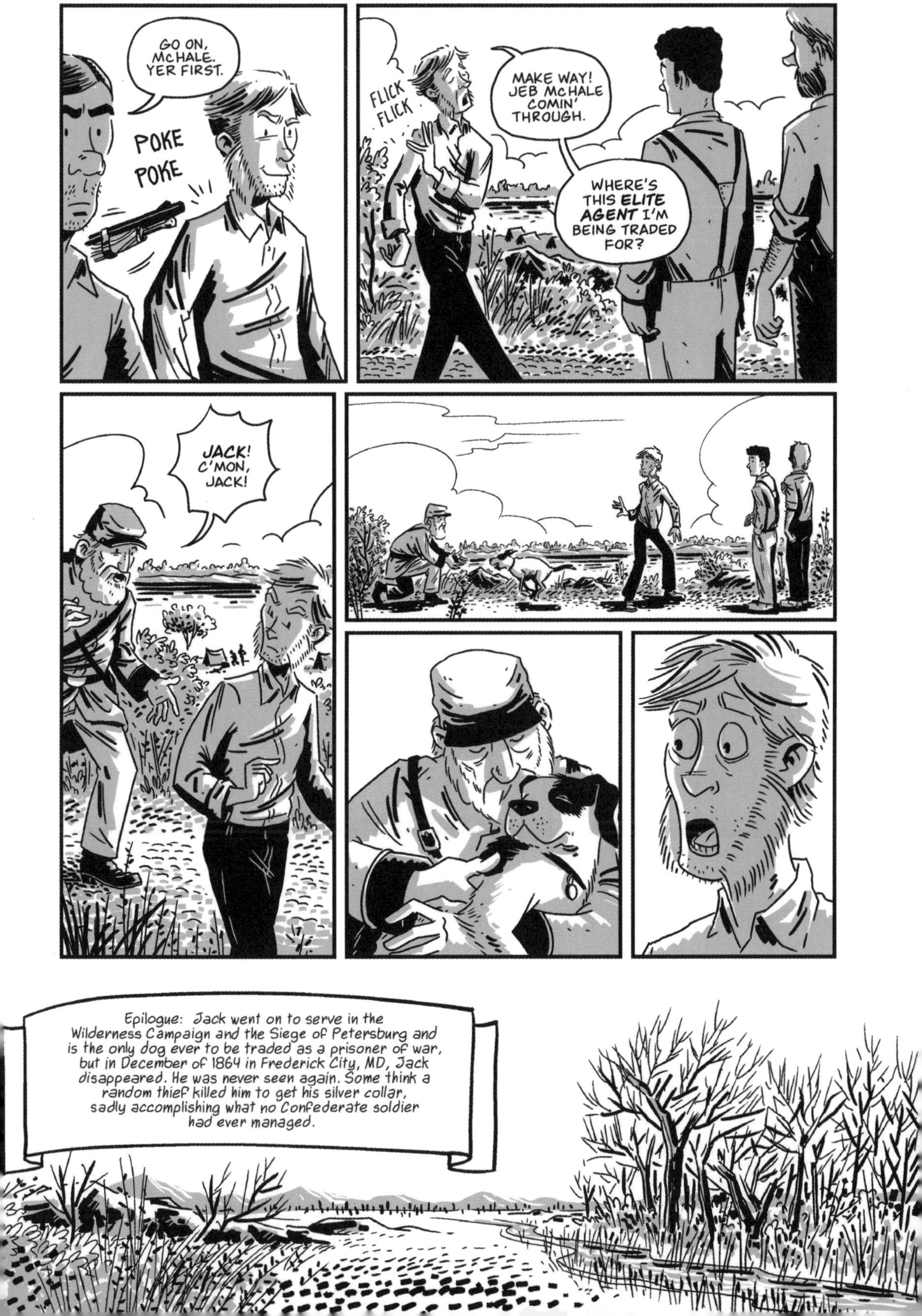
GO ON, McHALE. YER FIRST.
POKE POKE
FLICK FLICK
MAKE WAY! JEB McHALE COMIN' THROUGH.
WHERE'S THIS **ELITE AGENT** I'M BEING TRADED FOR?
JACK! C'MON, JACK!
Epilogue: Jack went on to serve in the Wilderness Campaign and the Siege of Petersburg and is the only dog ever to be traded as a prisoner of war, but in December of 1864 in Frederick City, MD, Jack disappeared. He was never seen again. Some think a random thief killed him to get his silver collar, sadly accomplishing what no Confederate soldier had ever managed.

SHIPS' CATS

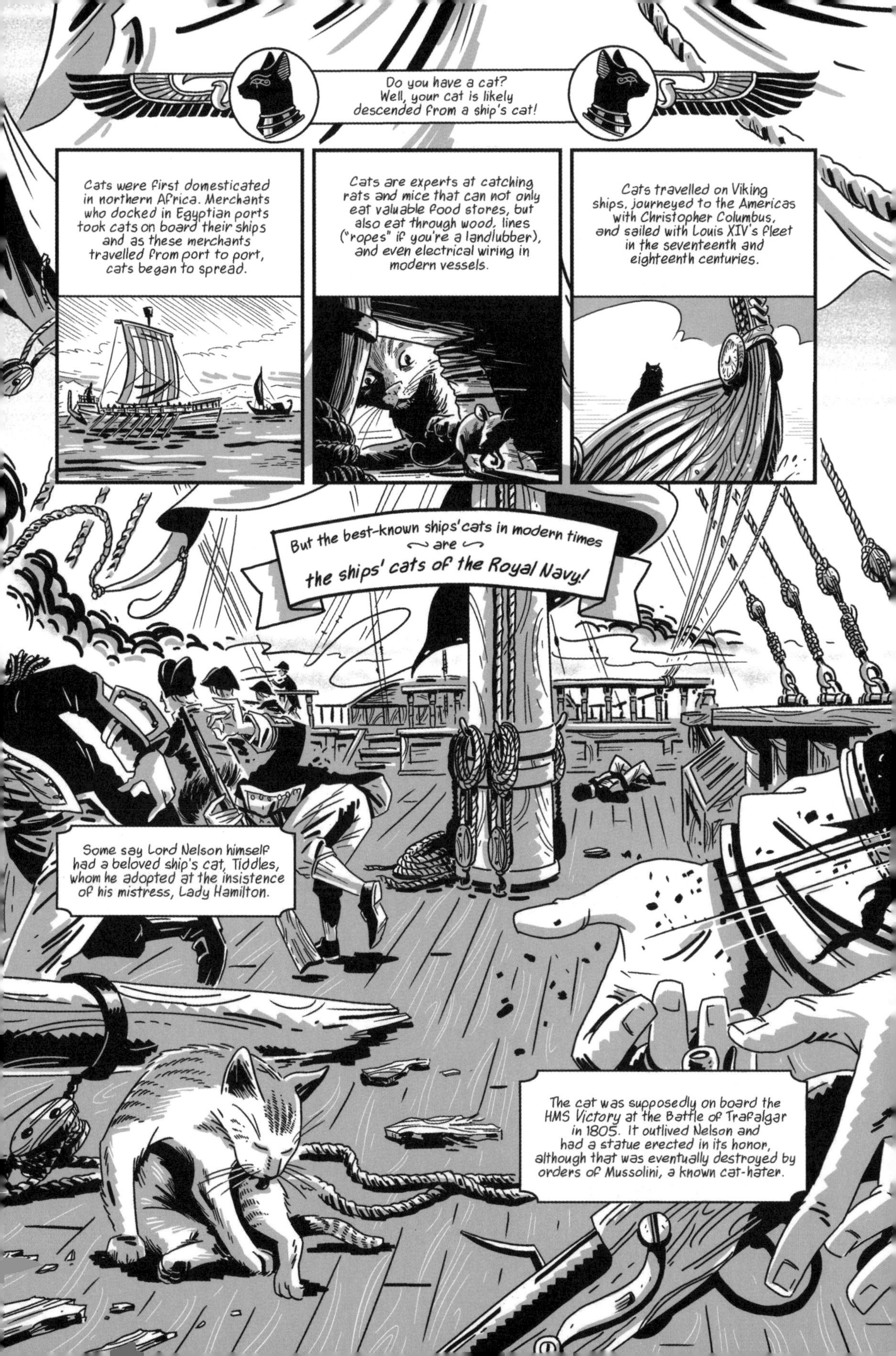
Do you have a cat? Well, your cat is likely descended from a ship's cat!
Cats were first domesticated in northern Africa. Merchants who docked in Egyptian ports took cats on board their ships and as these merchants travelled from port to port, cats began to spread.
Cats are experts at catching rats and mice that can not only eat valuable food stores, but also eat through wood, lines ("ropes" if you're a landlubber), and even electrical wiring in modern vessels.
Cats travelled on Viking ships, journeyed to the Americas with Christopher Columbus, and sailed with Louis XIV's fleet in the seventeenth and eighteenth centuries.
But the best-known ships' cats in modern times are the ships' cats of the Royal Navy!
Some say Lord Nelson himself had a beloved ship's cat, Tiddles, whom he adopted at the insistence of his mistress, Lady Hamilton.
The cat was supposedly on board the HMS Victory at the Battle of Trafalgar in 1805. It outlived Nelson and had a statue erected in its honor, although that was eventually destroyed by orders of Mussolini, a known cat-hater.

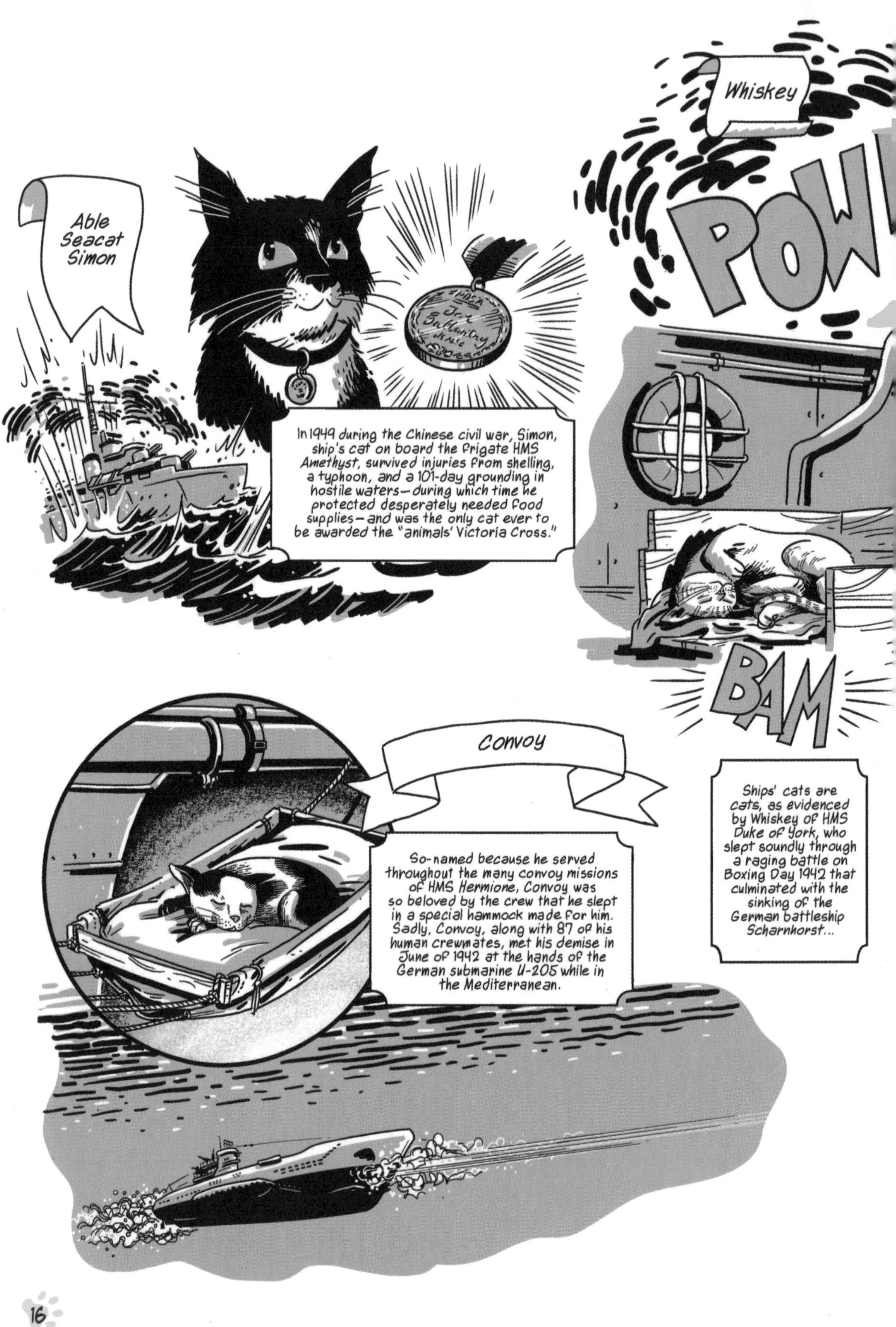

Able Seacat Simon
In 1949 during the Chinese civil war, Simon, ship's cat on board the frigate HMS Amethyst, survived injuries from shelling, a typhoon, and a 101-day grounding in hostile waters—during which time he protected desperately needed food supplies—and was the only cat ever to be awarded the "animals' Victoria Cross."
Whiskey
POW
BAM
Ships' cats are cats, as evidenced by Whiskey of HMS Duke of York, who slept soundly through a raging battle on Boxing Day 1942 that culminated with the sinking of the German battleship Scharnhorst...
Convoy
So-named because he served throughout the many convoy missions of HMS Hermione, Convoy was so beloved by the crew that he slept in a special hammock made for him. Sadly, Convoy, along with 87 of his human crewmates, met his demise in June of 1942 at the hands of the German submarine U-205 while in the Mediterranean.

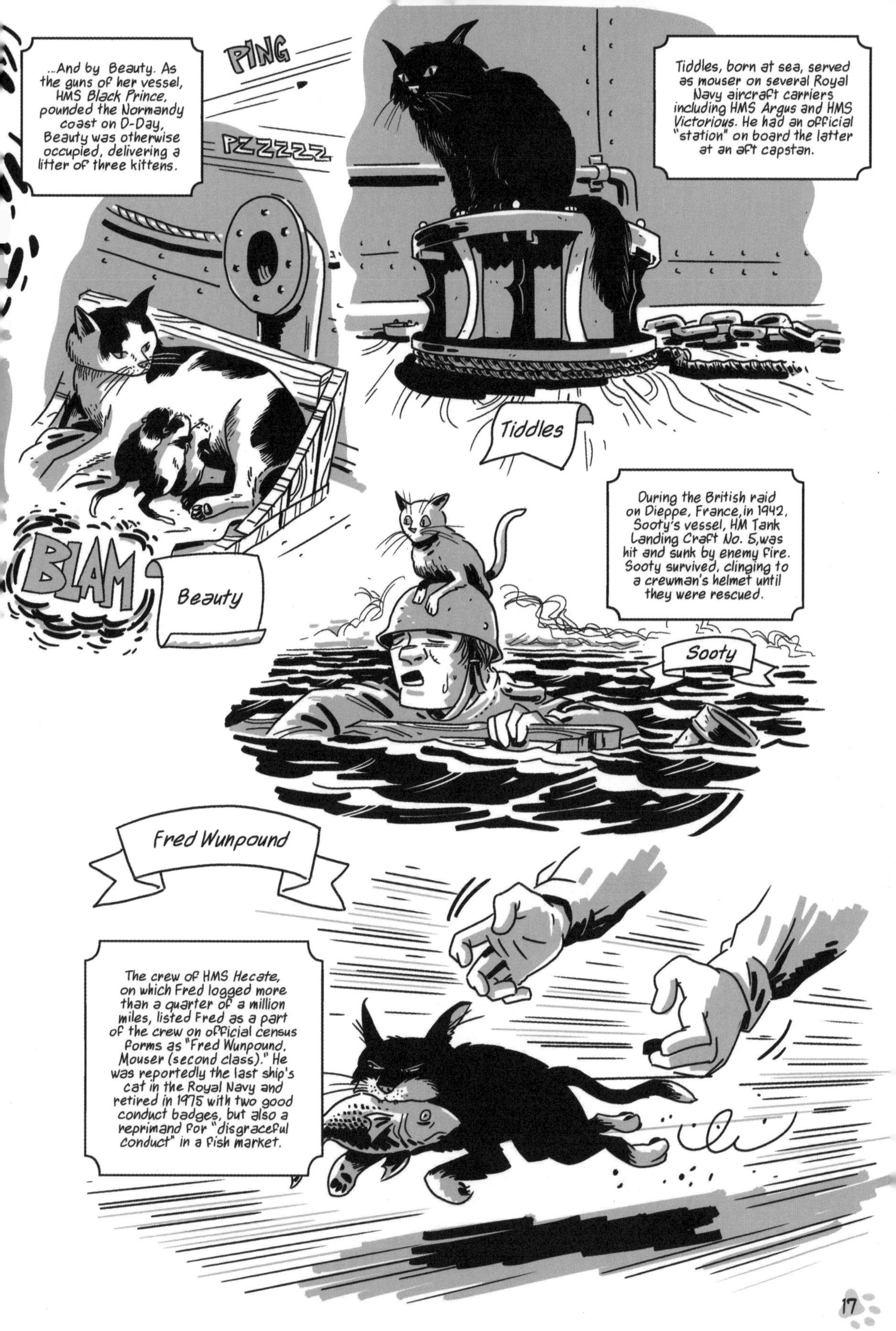
...And by Beauty. As the guns of her vessel, HMS Black Prince, pounded the Normandy coast on D-Day, Beauty was otherwise occupied, delivering a litter of three kittens.
PING
PZZZZZ
BLAM
Beauty
Tiddles, born at sea, served as mouser on several Royal Navy aircraft carriers including HMS Argus and HMS Victorious. He had an official "station" on board the latter at an aft capstan.
Tiddles
During the British raid on Dieppe, France, in 1942, Sooty's vessel, HM Tank Landing Craft No. 5, was hit and sunk by enemy fire. Sooty survived, clinging to a crewman's helmet until they were rescued.
Sooty
Fred Wunpound
The crew of HMS Hecate, on which Fred logged more than a quarter of a million miles, listed Fred as a part of the crew on official census forms as "Fred Wunpound, Mouser (second class)." He was reportedly the last ship's cat in the Royal Navy and retired in 1975 with two good conduct badges, but also a reprimand for "disgraceful conduct" in a fish market.

DOLPHINS

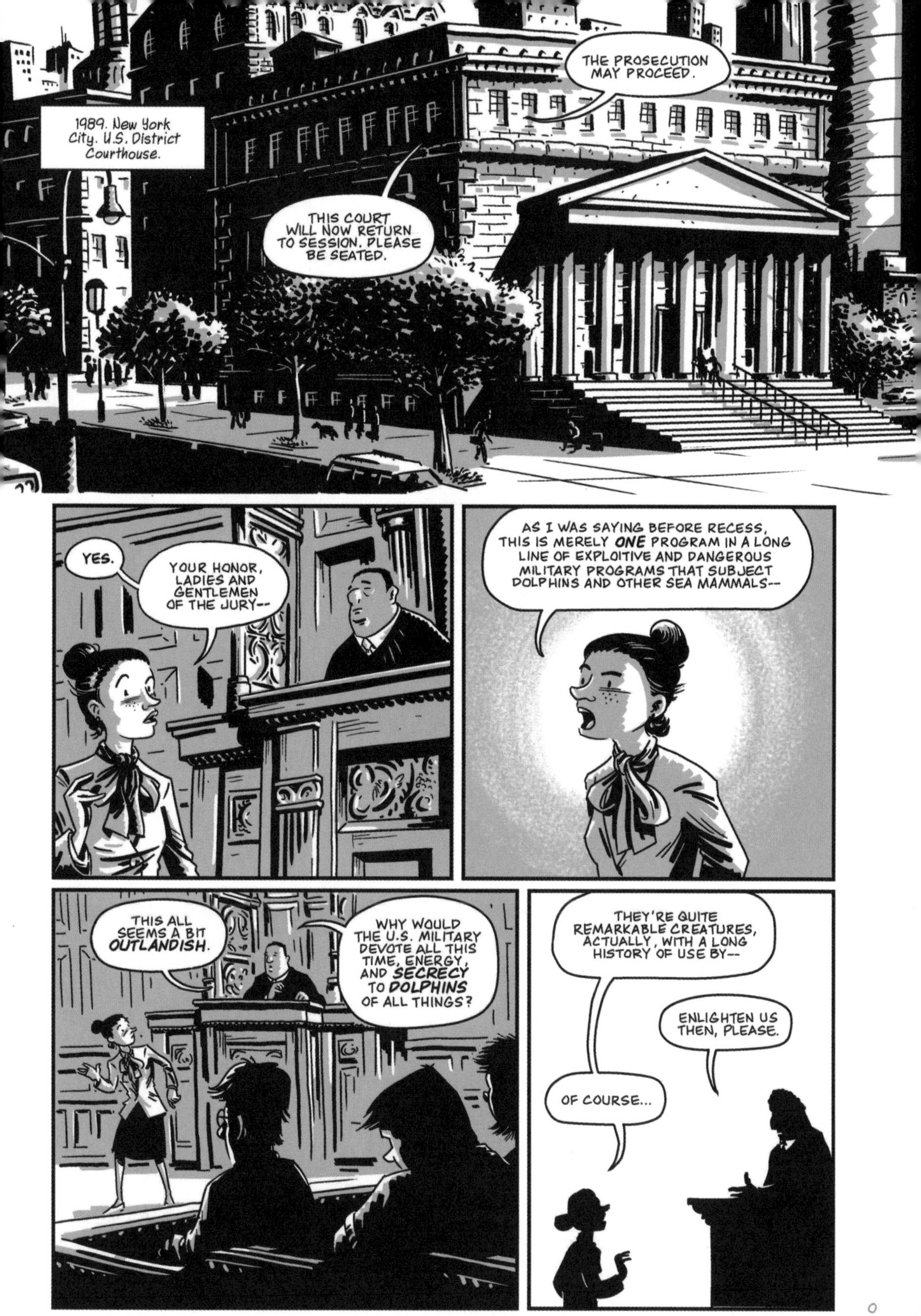

1989. New York City. U.S. District Courthouse.
THE PROSECUTION MAY PROCEED.
THIS COURT WILL NOW RETURN TO SESSION. PLEASE BE SEATED.
YES.
YOUR HONOR, LADIES AND GENTLEMEN OF THE JURY--
AS I WAS SAYING BEFORE RECESS, THIS IS MERELY ONE PROGRAM IN A LONG LINE OF EXPLOITIVE AND DANGEROUS MILITARY PROGRAMS THAT SUBJECT DOLPHINS AND OTHER SEA MAMMALS--
THIS ALL SEEMS A BIT OUTLANDISH.
WHY WOULD THE U.S. MILITARY DEVOTE ALL THIS TIME, ENERGY, AND SECRECY TO DOLPHINS OF ALL THINGS?
THEY'RE QUITE REMARKABLE CREATURES, ACTUALLY, WITH A LONG HISTORY OF USE BY--
ENLIGHTEN US THEN, PLEASE.
OF COURSE...

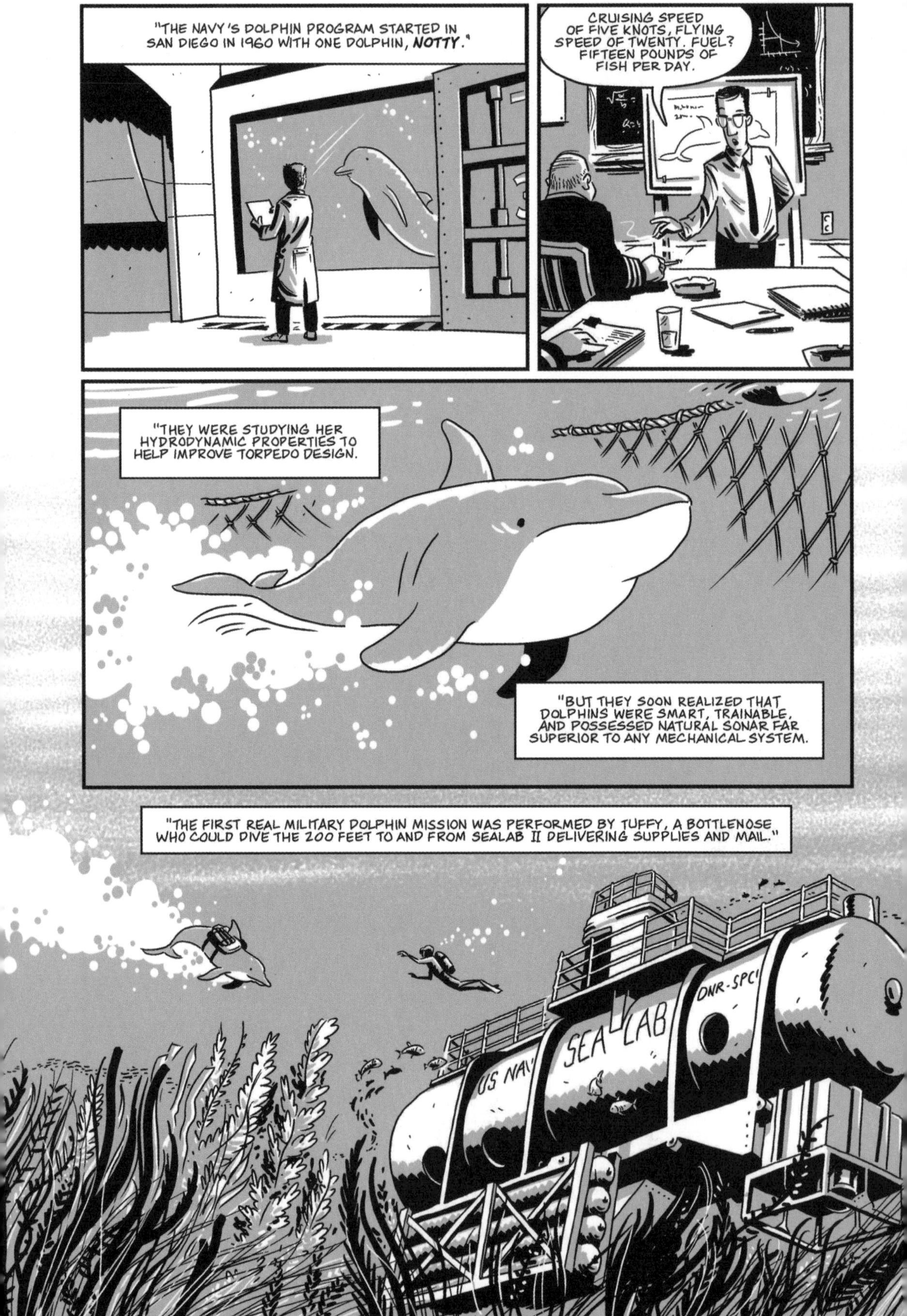
"THE NAVY'S DOLPHIN PROGRAM STARTED IN SAN DIEGO IN 1960 WITH ONE DOLPHIN, **NOTTY**."
CRUISING SPEED OF FIVE KNOTS, FLYING SPEED OF TWENTY. FUEL? FIFTEEN POUNDS OF FISH PER DAY.
"THEY WERE STUDYING HER HYDRODYNAMIC PROPERTIES TO HELP IMPROVE TORPEDO DESIGN.
"BUT THEY SOON REALIZED THAT DOLPHINS WERE SMART, TRAINABLE, AND POSSESSED NATURAL SONAR FAR SUPERIOR TO ANY MECHANICAL SYSTEM.
"THE FIRST REAL MILITARY DOLPHIN MISSION WAS PERFORMED BY TUFFY, A BOTTLENOSE WHO COULD DIVE THE 200 FEET TO AND FROM SEALAB II DELIVERING SUPPLIES AND MAIL."
US NAV
SEA LAB
DNR-SPC

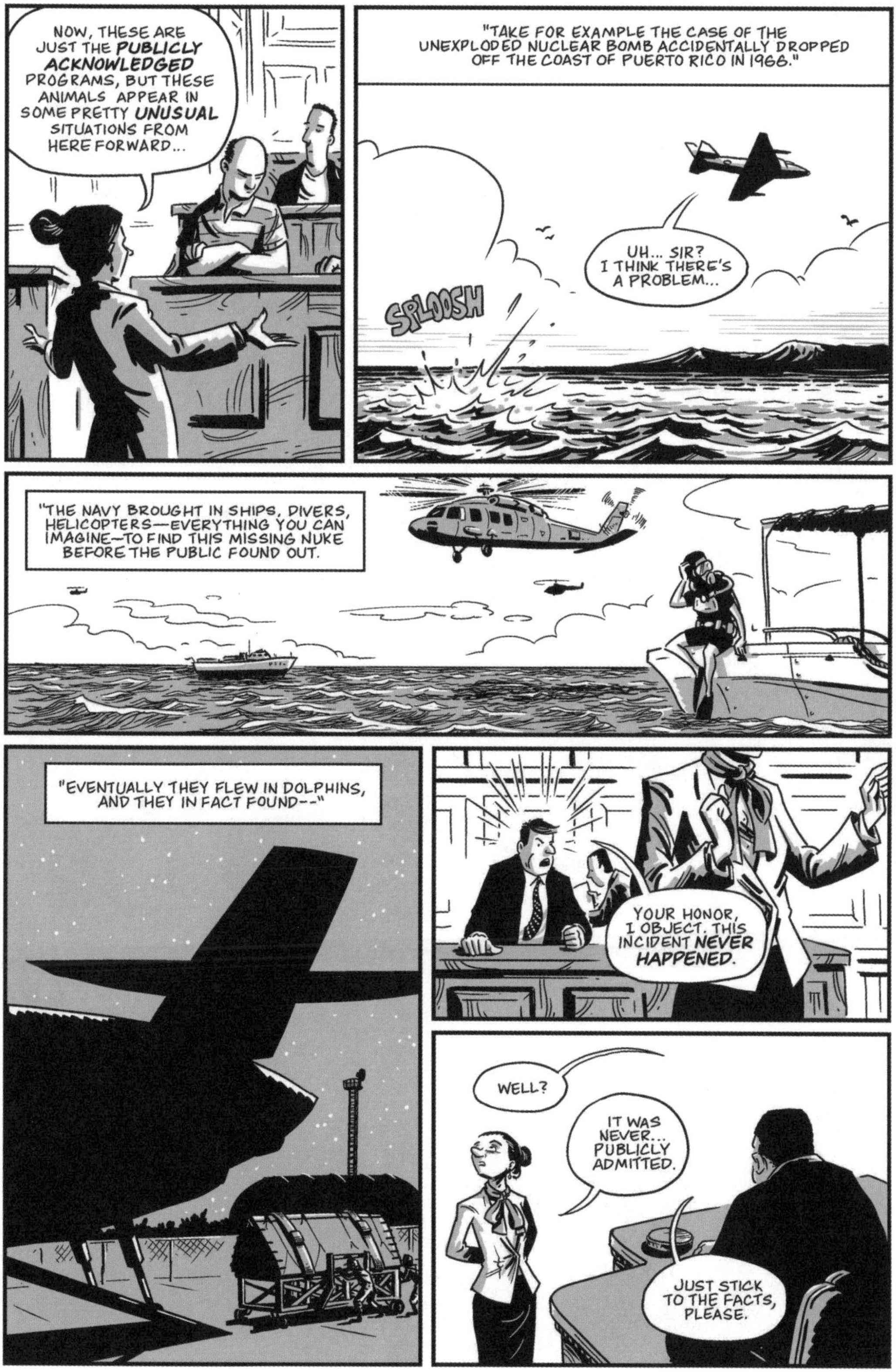

NOW, THESE ARE JUST THE **PUBLICLY ACKNOWLEDGED** PROGRAMS, BUT THESE ANIMALS APPEAR IN SOME PRETTY **UNUSUAL** SITUATIONS FROM HERE FORWARD...
"TAKE FOR EXAMPLE THE CASE OF THE UNEXPLODED NUCLEAR BOMB ACCIDENTALLY DROPPED OFF THE COAST OF PUERTO RICO IN 1966."
UH... SIR? I THINK THERE'S A PROBLEM...
SPLOOSH
"THE NAVY BROUGHT IN SHIPS, DIVERS, HELICOPTERS—EVERYTHING YOU CAN IMAGINE—TO FIND THIS MISSING NUKE BEFORE THE PUBLIC FOUND OUT.
"EVENTUALLY THEY FLEW IN DOLPHINS, AND THEY IN FACT FOUND--"
YOUR HONOR, I OBJECT. THIS INCIDENT **NEVER HAPPENED**.
WELL?
IT WAS NEVER... PUBLICLY ADMITTED.
JUST STICK TO THE FACTS, PLEASE.

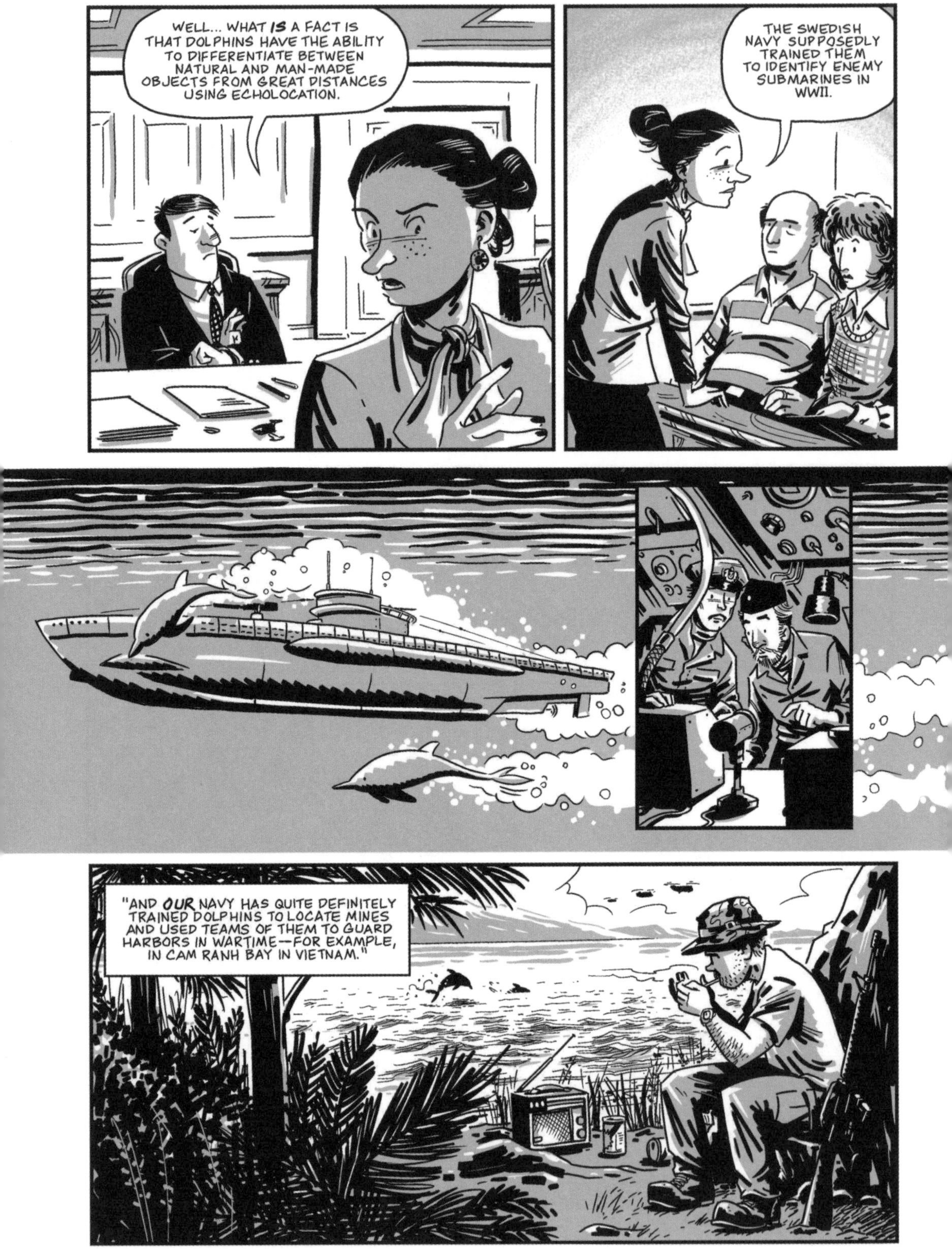
WELL... WHAT IS A FACT IS THAT DOLPHINS HAVE THE ABILITY TO DIFFERENTIATE BETWEEN NATURAL AND MAN-MADE OBJECTS FROM GREAT DISTANCES USING ECHOLOCATION.
THE SWEDISH NAVY SUPPOSEDLY TRAINED THEM TO IDENTIFY ENEMY SUBMARINES IN WWII.
"AND OUR NAVY HAS QUITE DEFINITELY TRAINED DOLPHINS TO LOCATE MINES AND USED TEAMS OF THEM TO GUARD HARBORS IN WARTIME—FOR EXAMPLE, IN CAM RANH BAY IN VIETNAM."

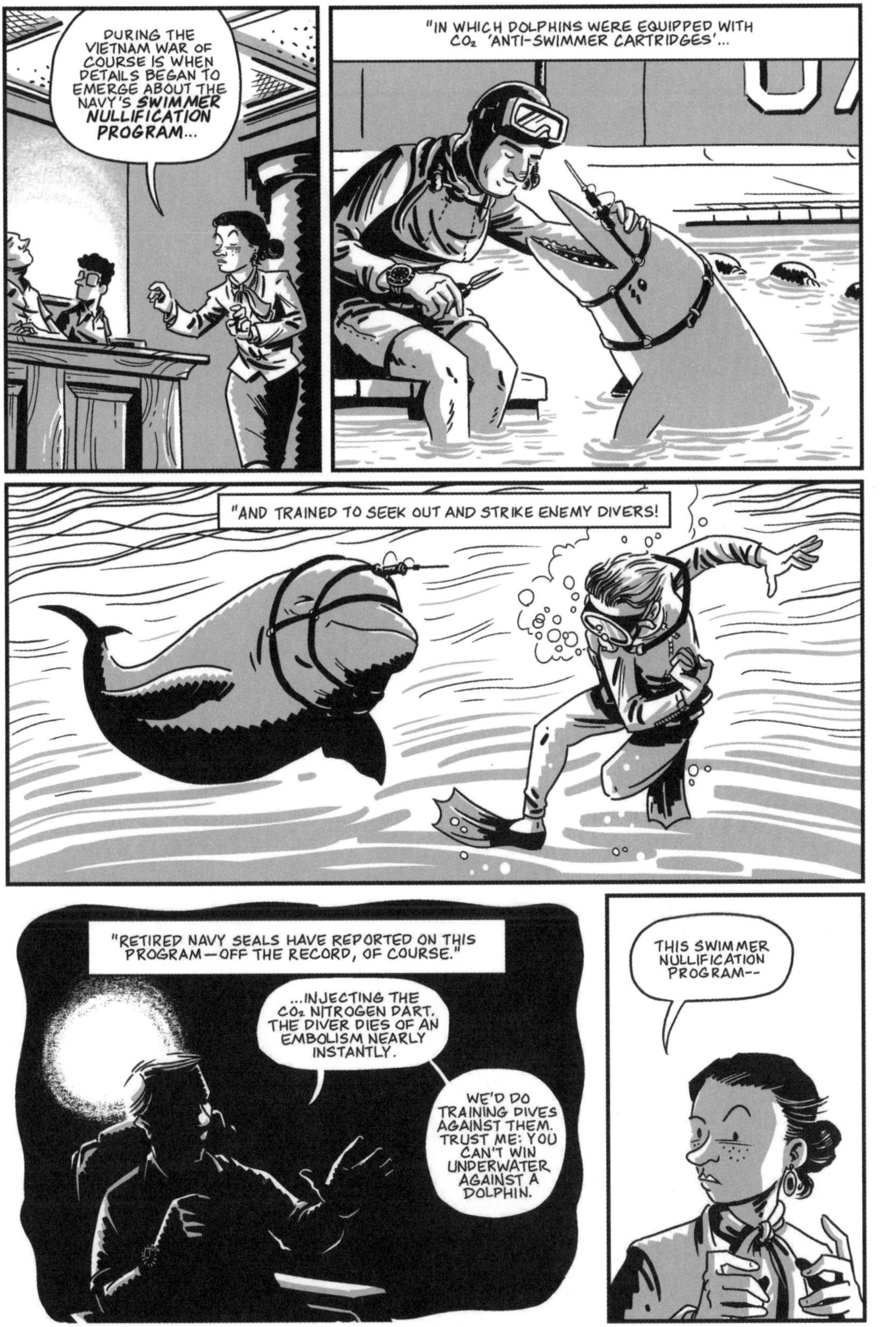
DURING THE VIETNAM WAR OF COURSE IS WHEN DETAILS BEGAN TO EMERGE ABOUT THE NAVY'S SWIMMER NULLIFICATION PROGRAM...
"IN WHICH DOLPHINS WERE EQUIPPED WITH CO_2 'ANTI-SWIMMER CARTRIDGES'...
"AND TRAINED TO SEEK OUT AND STRIKE ENEMY DIVERS!
"RETIRED NAVY SEALS HAVE REPORTED ON THIS PROGRAM—OFF THE RECORD, OF COURSE."
...INJECTING THE CO_2 NITROGEN DART. THE DIVER DIES OF AN EMBOLISM NEARLY INSTANTLY.
WE'D DO TRAINING DIVES AGAINST THEM. TRUST ME: YOU CAN'T WIN UNDERWATER AGAINST A DOLPHIN.
THIS SWIMMER NULLIFICATION PROGRAM--

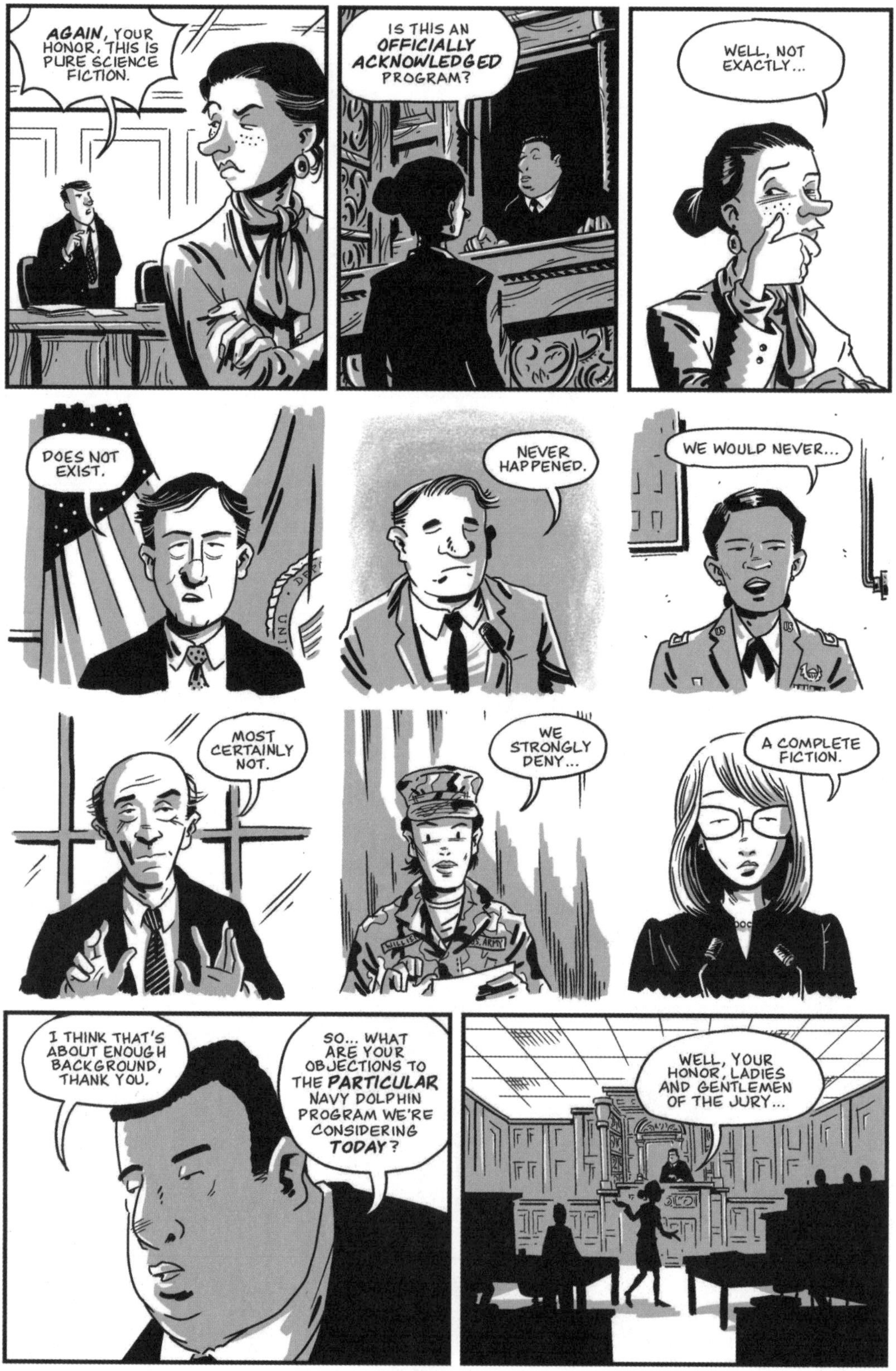
AGAIN, YOUR HONOR, THIS IS PURE SCIENCE FICTION.
IS THIS AN OFFICIALLY ACKNOWLEDGED PROGRAM?
WELL, NOT EXACTLY...
DOES NOT EXIST.
NEVER HAPPENED.
WE WOULD NEVER...
MOST CERTAINLY NOT.
WE STRONGLY DENY...
A COMPLETE FICTION.
I THINK THAT'S ABOUT ENOUGH BACKGROUND, THANK YOU.
SO... WHAT ARE YOUR OBJECTIONS TO THE PARTICULAR NAVY DOLPHIN PROGRAM WE'RE CONSIDERING TODAY?
WELL, YOUR HONOR, LADIES AND GENTLEMEN OF THE JURY...

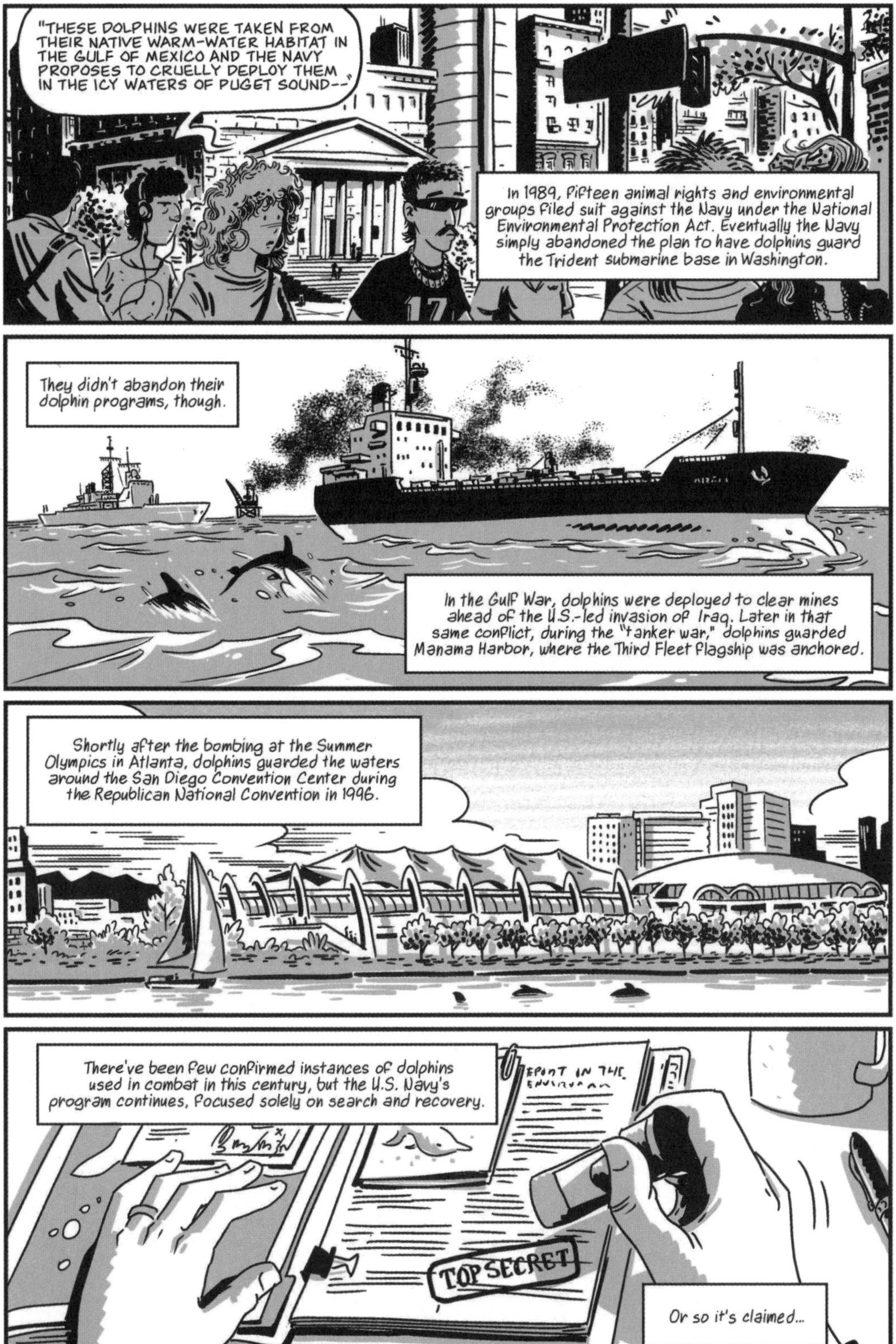
"THESE DOLPHINS WERE TAKEN FROM THEIR NATIVE WARM-WATER HABITAT IN THE GULF OF MEXICO AND THE NAVY PROPOSES TO CRUELLY DEPLOY THEM IN THE ICY WATERS OF PUGET SOUND--"
In 1989, fifteen animal rights and environmental groups filed suit against the Navy under the National Environmental Protection Act. Eventually the Navy simply abandoned the plan to have dolphins guard the Trident submarine base in Washington.
They didn't abandon their dolphin programs, though.
In the Gulf War, dolphins were deployed to clear mines ahead of the U.S.-led invasion of Iraq. Later in that same conflict, during the "tanker war," dolphins guarded Manama Harbor, where the Third Fleet flagship was anchored.
Shortly after the bombing at the Summer Olympics in Atlanta, dolphins guarded the waters around the San Diego Convention Center during the Republican National Convention in 1996.
There've been few confirmed instances of dolphins used in combat in this century, but the U.S. Navy's program continues, focused solely on search and recovery.
TOP SECRET
Or so it's claimed...

MASCOTS

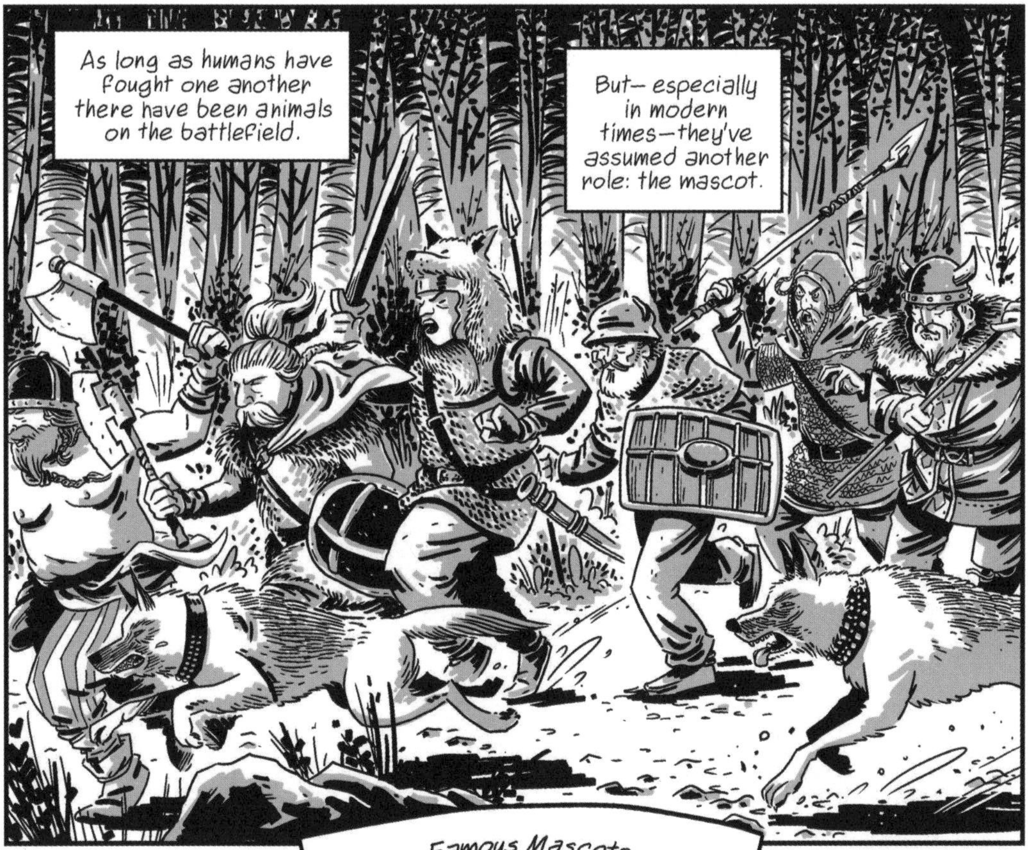
As long as humans have fought one another there have been animals on the battlefield.
But— especially in modern times—they've assumed another role: the mascot.

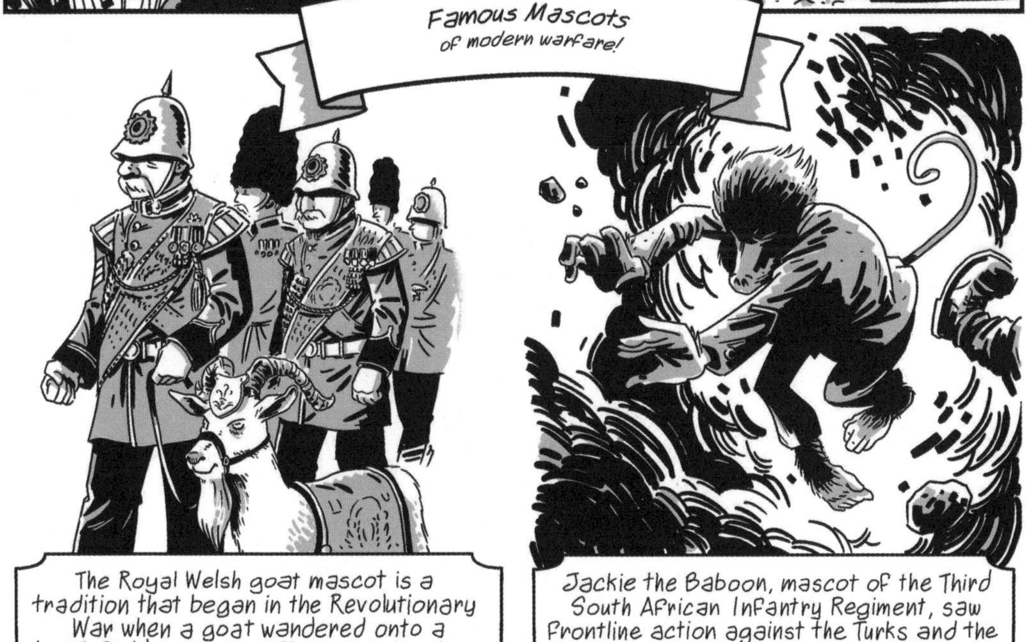
Famous Mascots
of modern warfare!
The Royal Welsh goat mascot is a tradition that began in the Revolutionary War when a goat wandered onto a battlefield in Boston. Since then they've had an unbroken chain of Kashmir goat mascots, all named William (AKA "Billy").
Jackie the Baboon, mascot of the Third South African Infantry Regiment, saw frontline action against the Turks and the Germans and fought in Egypt and France. He returned from WWI with the rank of corporal, but without his right leg.

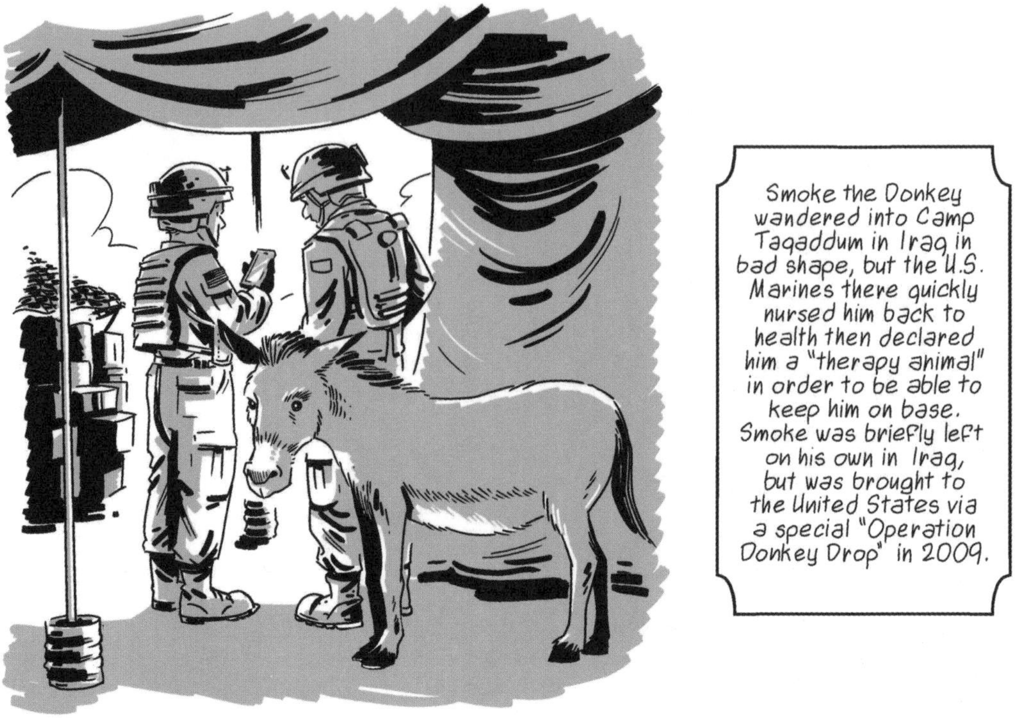
Smoke the Donkey wandered into Camp Taqaddum in Iraq in bad shape, but the U.S. Marines there quickly nursed him back to health then declared him a "therapy animal" in order to be able to keep him on base. Smoke was briefly left on his own in Iraq, but was brought to the United States via a special "Operation Donkey Drop" in 2009.

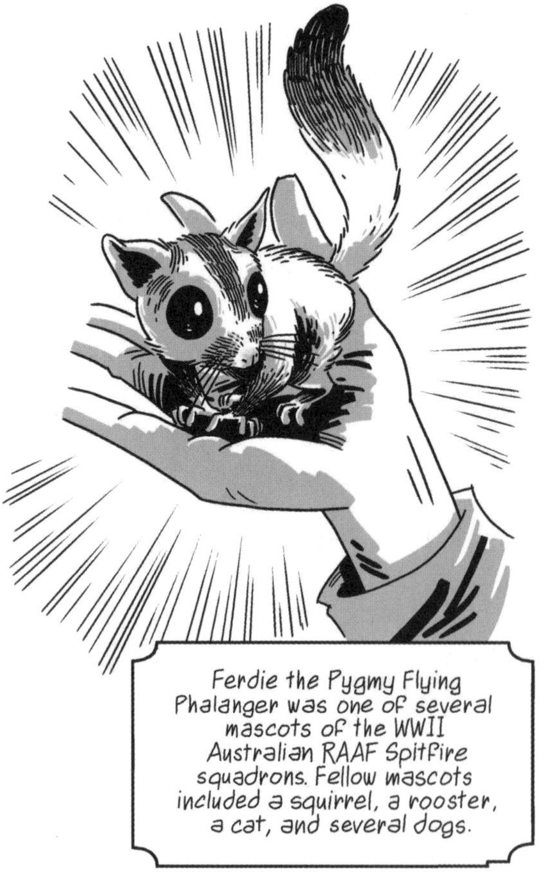
Ferdie the Pygmy Flying Phalanger was one of several mascots of the WWII Australian RAAF Spitfire squadrons. Fellow mascots included a squirrel, a rooster, a cat, and several dogs.

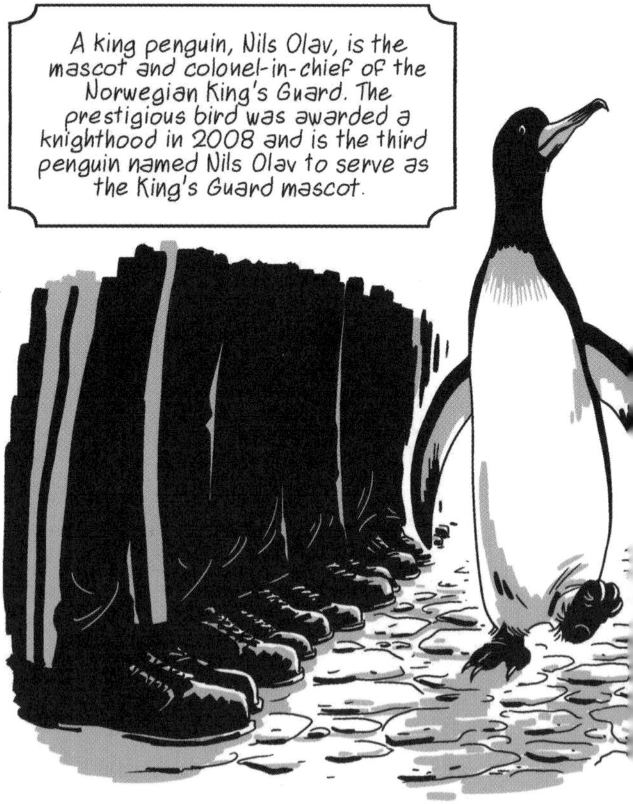
A king penguin, Nils Olav, is the mascot and colonel-in-chief of the Norwegian King's Guard. The prestigious bird was awarded a knighthood in 2008 and is the third penguin named Nils Olav to serve as the King's Guard mascot.

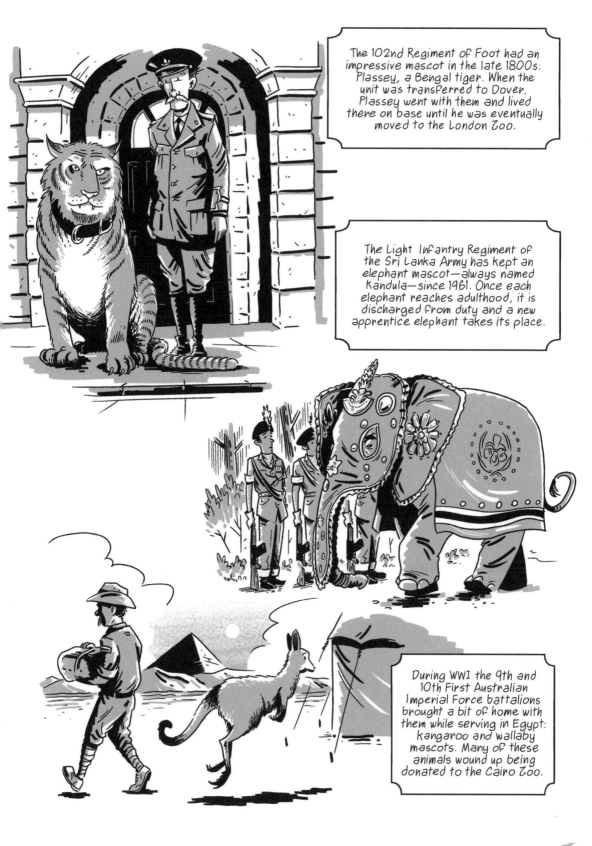

The 102nd Regiment of Foot had an impressive mascot in the late 1800s: Plassey, a Bengal tiger. When the unit was transferred to Dover, Plassey went with them and lived there on base until he was eventually moved to the London Zoo.

The Light Infantry Regiment of the Sri Lanka Army has kept an elephant mascot—always named Kandula—since 1961. Once each elephant reaches adulthood, it is discharged from duty and a new apprentice elephant takes its place.

During WWI the 9th and 10th First Australian Imperial Force battalions brought a bit of home with them while serving in Egypt: kangaroo and wallaby mascots. Many of these animals wound up being donated to the Cairo Zoo.

SATAN

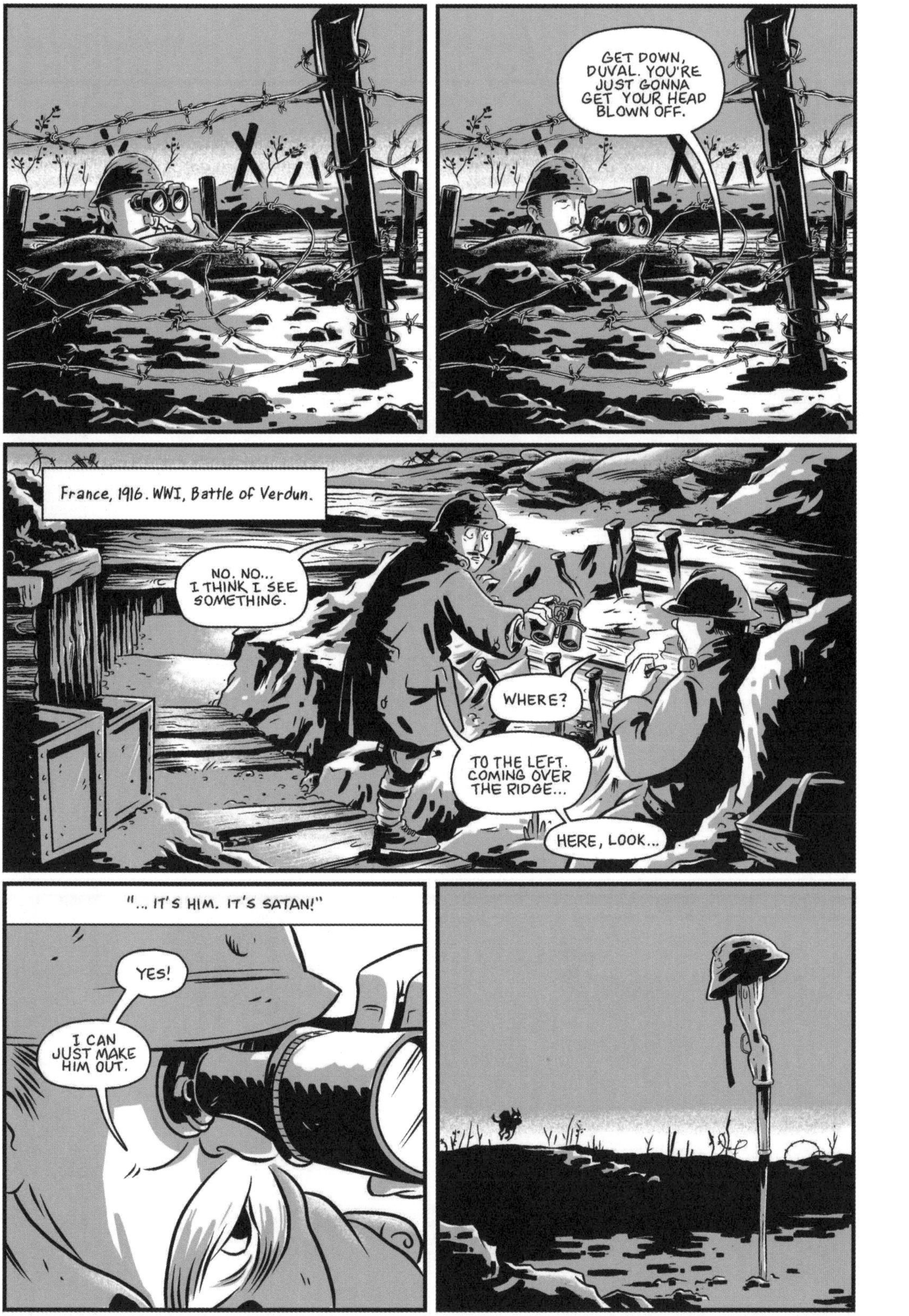
GET DOWN, DUVAL. YOU'RE JUST GONNA GET YOUR HEAD BLOWN OFF.
France, 1916. WWI, Battle of Verdun.
NO. NO... I THINK I SEE SOMETHING.
WHERE?
TO THE LEFT. COMING OVER THE RIDGE...
HERE, LOOK...
"... IT'S HIM. IT'S SATAN!"
YES!
I CAN JUST MAKE HIM OUT.

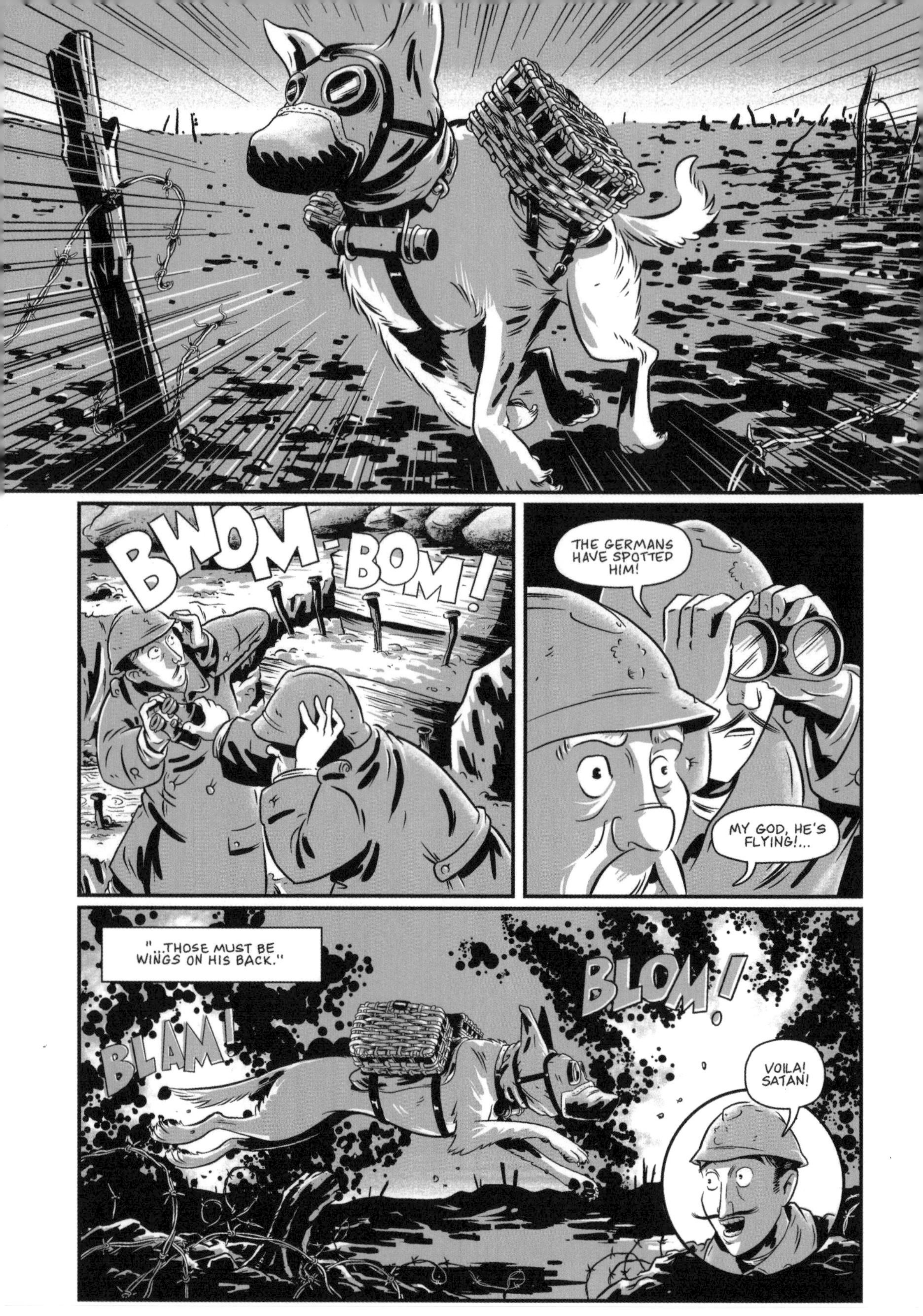
BWOM-BOM!
THE GERMANS HAVE SPOTTED HIM!
MY GOD, HE'S FLYING!...
"...THOSE MUST BE WINGS ON HIS BACK."
BLOM!
BLAM!
VOILA! SATAN!

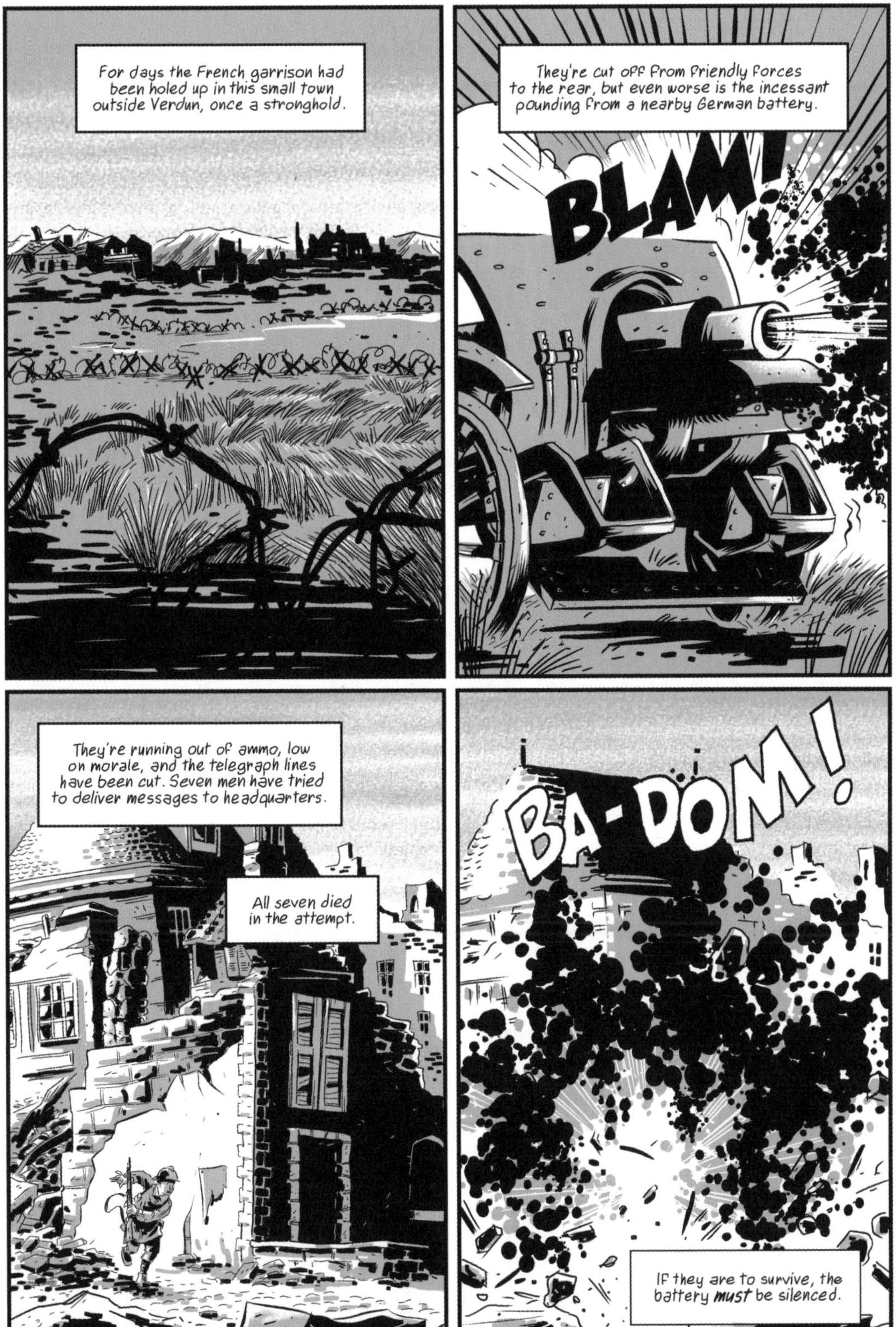
For days the French garrison had been holed up in this small town outside Verdun, once a stronghold.
They're cut off from friendly forces to the rear, but even worse is the incessant pounding from a nearby German battery.
BLAM!
They're running out of ammo, low on morale, and the telegraph lines have been cut. Seven men have tried to deliver messages to headquarters.
All seven died in the attempt.
BA-DOM!
If they are to survive, the battery *MUST* be silenced.

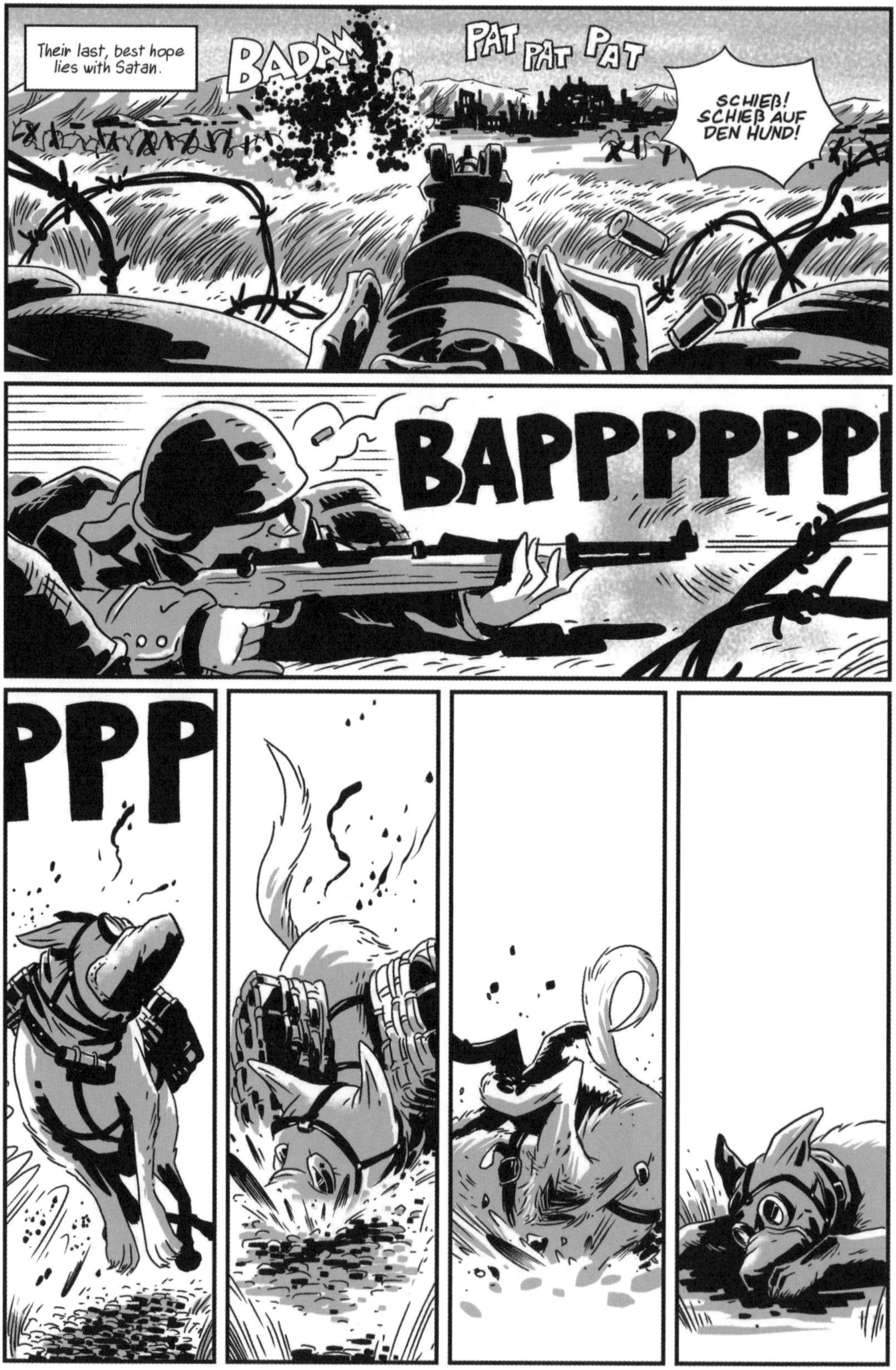
Their last, best hope lies with Satan.
BADAM
PAT PAT PAT
SCHIEß! SCHIEß AUF DEN HUND!
BAPPPPPPPPPP

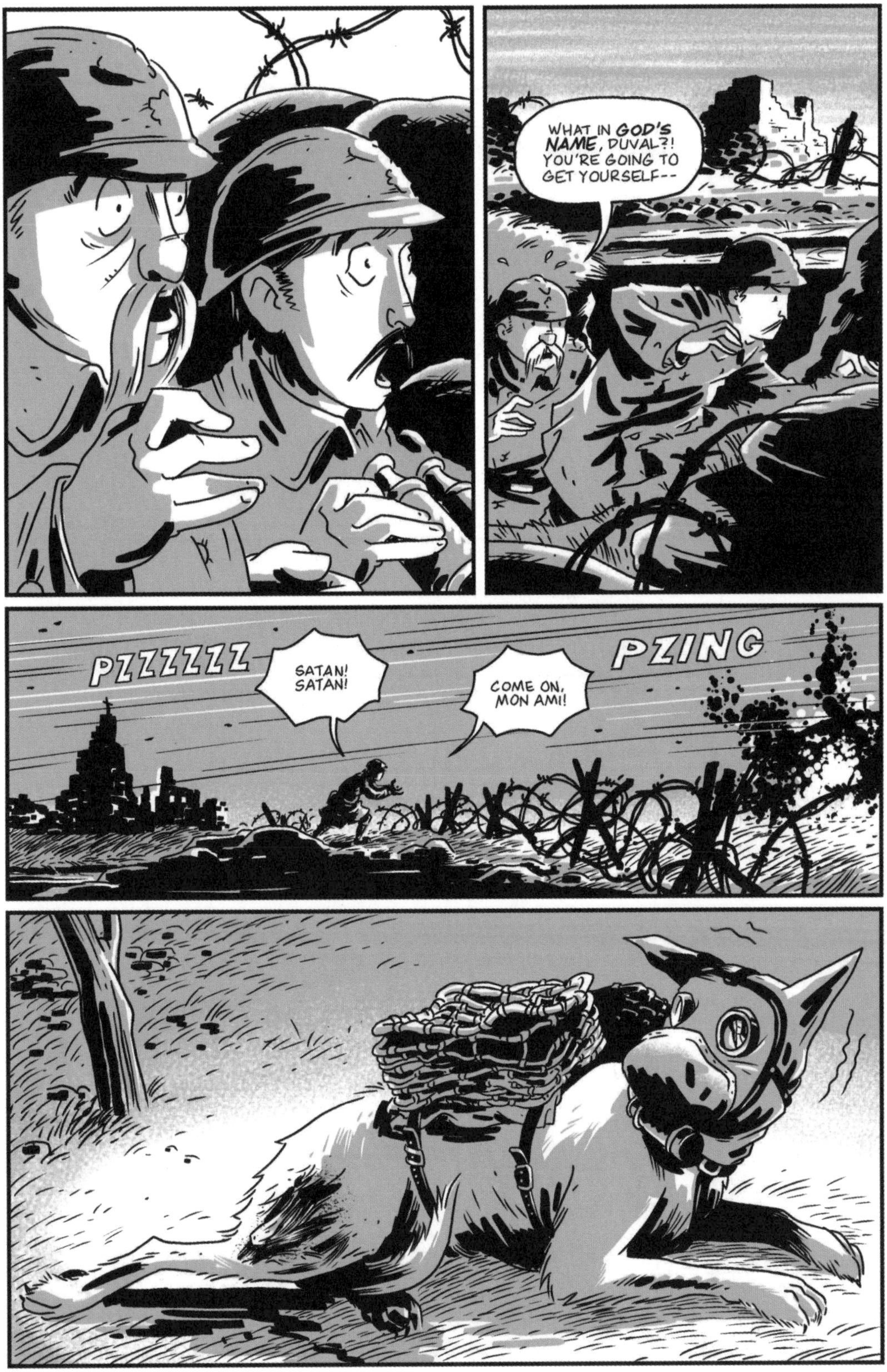
WHAT IN GOD'S NAME, DUVAL?! YOU'RE GOING TO GET YOURSELF--
PZZZZZZ
SATAN! SATAN!
COME ON, MON AMI!
PZING

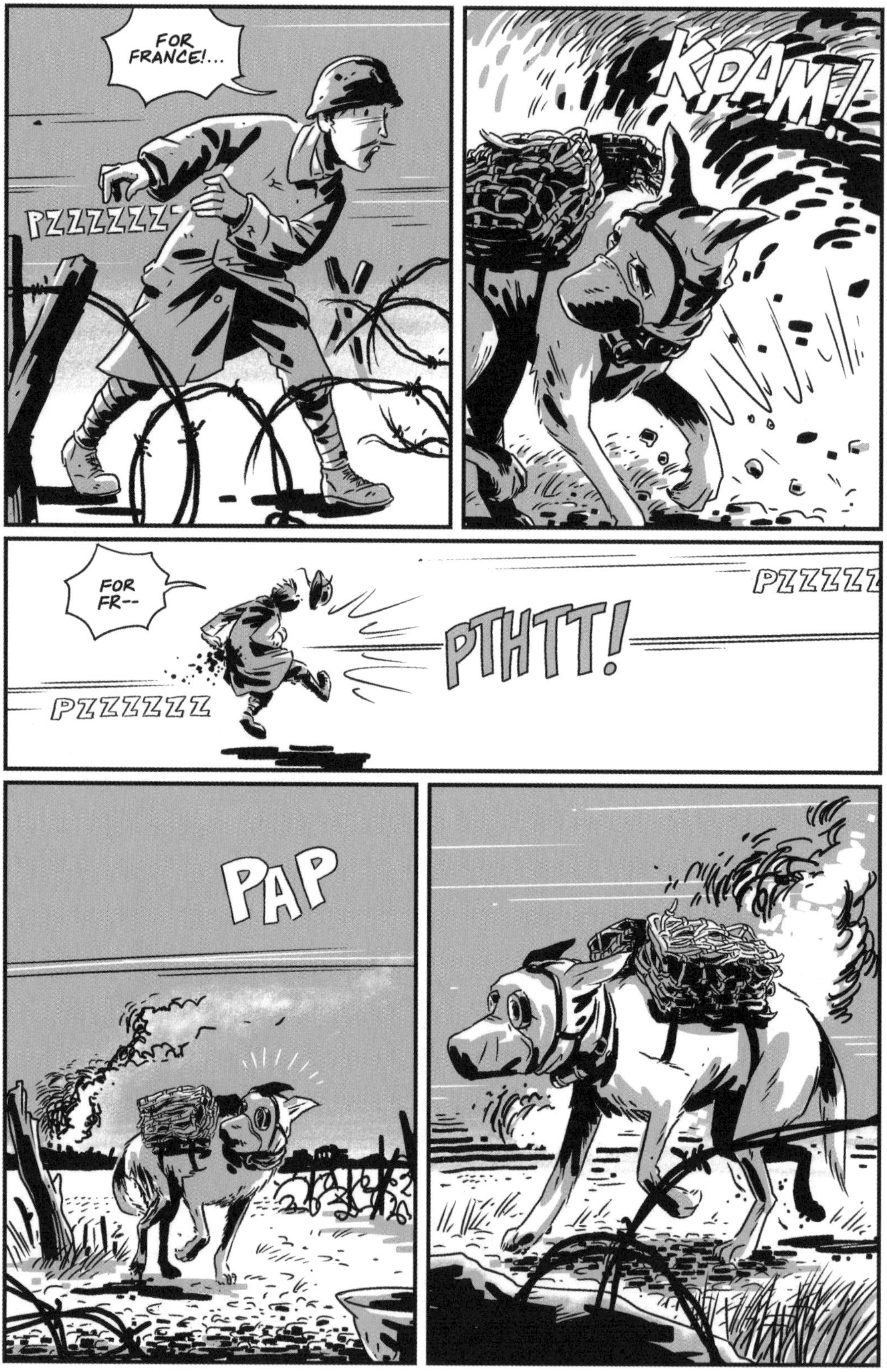
FOR FRANCE!...
PZZZZZZ
KPAM!
FOR FR--
PZZZZZ
PTHTT!
PZZZZZZ
PAP

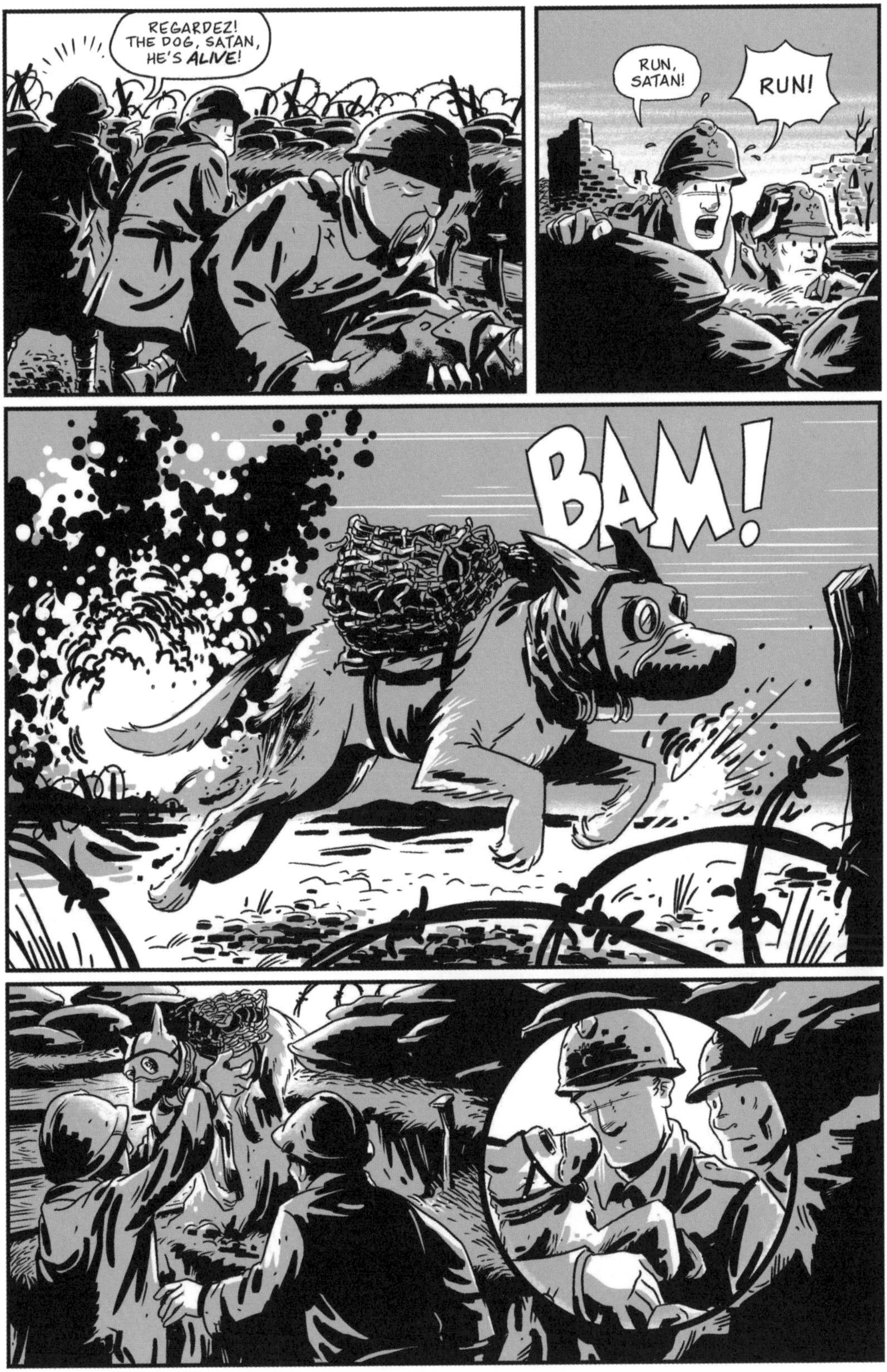
REGARDEZ! THE DOG, SATAN, HE'S ALIVE!
RUN, SATAN!
RUN!
BAM!

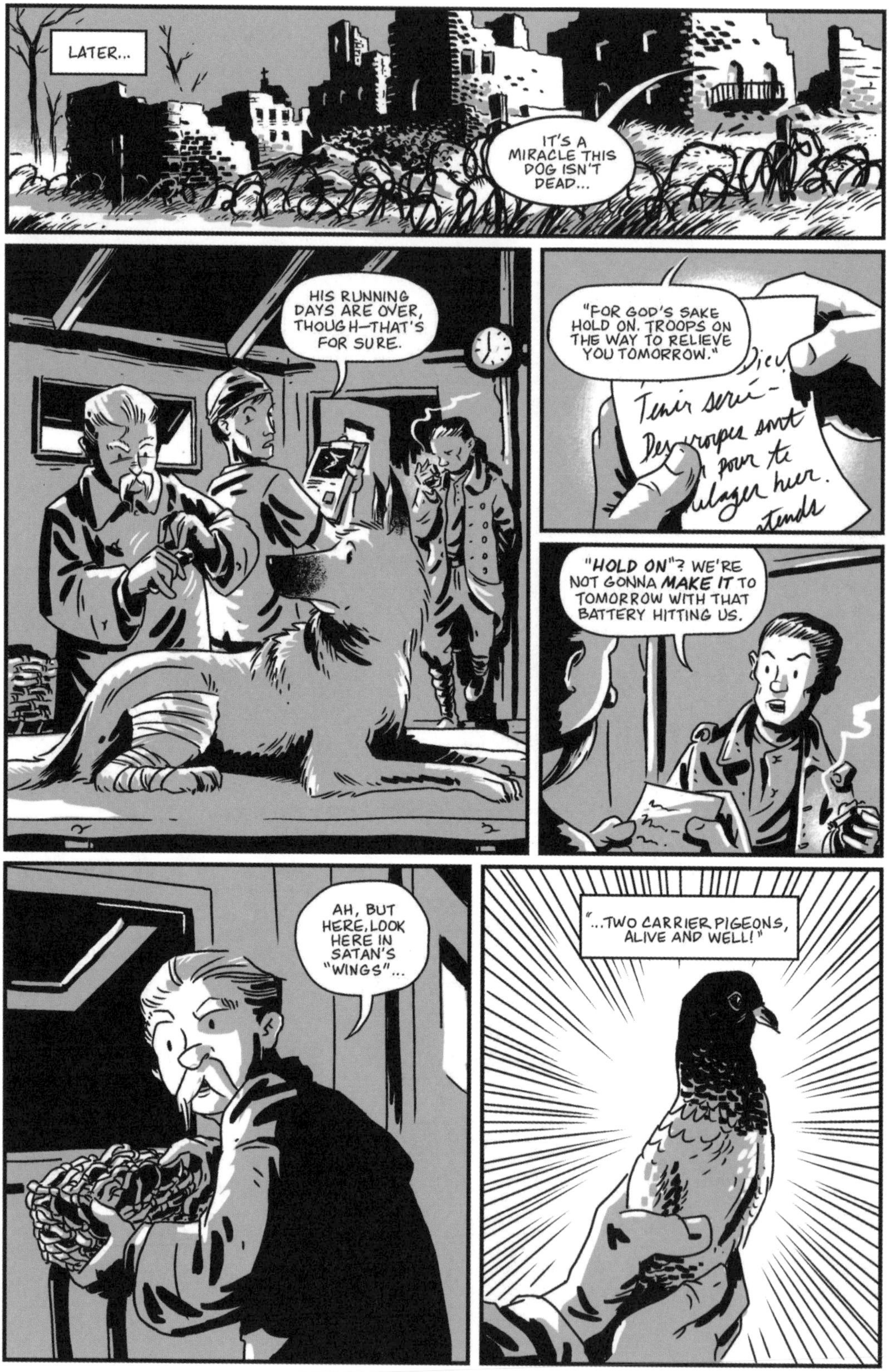
LATER...
IT'S A MIRACLE THIS DOG ISN'T DEAD...
HIS RUNNING DAYS ARE OVER, THOUGH—THAT'S FOR SURE.
"FOR GOD'S SAKE HOLD ON. TROOPS ON THE WAY TO RELIEVE YOU TOMORROW."
"HOLD ON"? WE'RE NOT GONNA MAKE IT TO TOMORROW WITH THAT BATTERY HITTING US.
AH, BUT HERE, LOOK HERE IN SATAN'S "WINGS"...
"...TWO CARRIER PIGEONS, ALIVE AND WELL!"

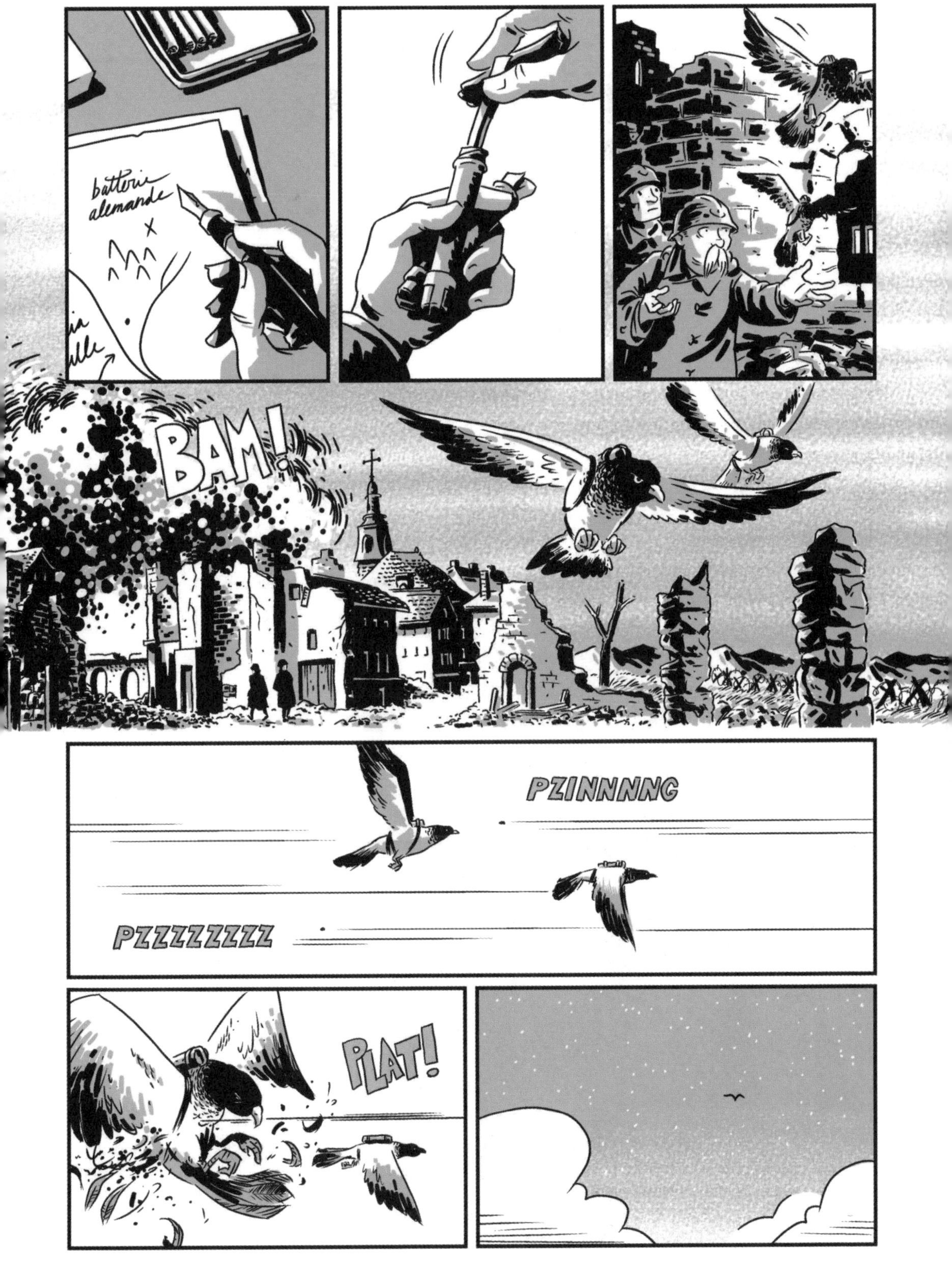
batterie
alemande
BAM!
PZINNNNG
PZZZZZZZZ
PLAT!

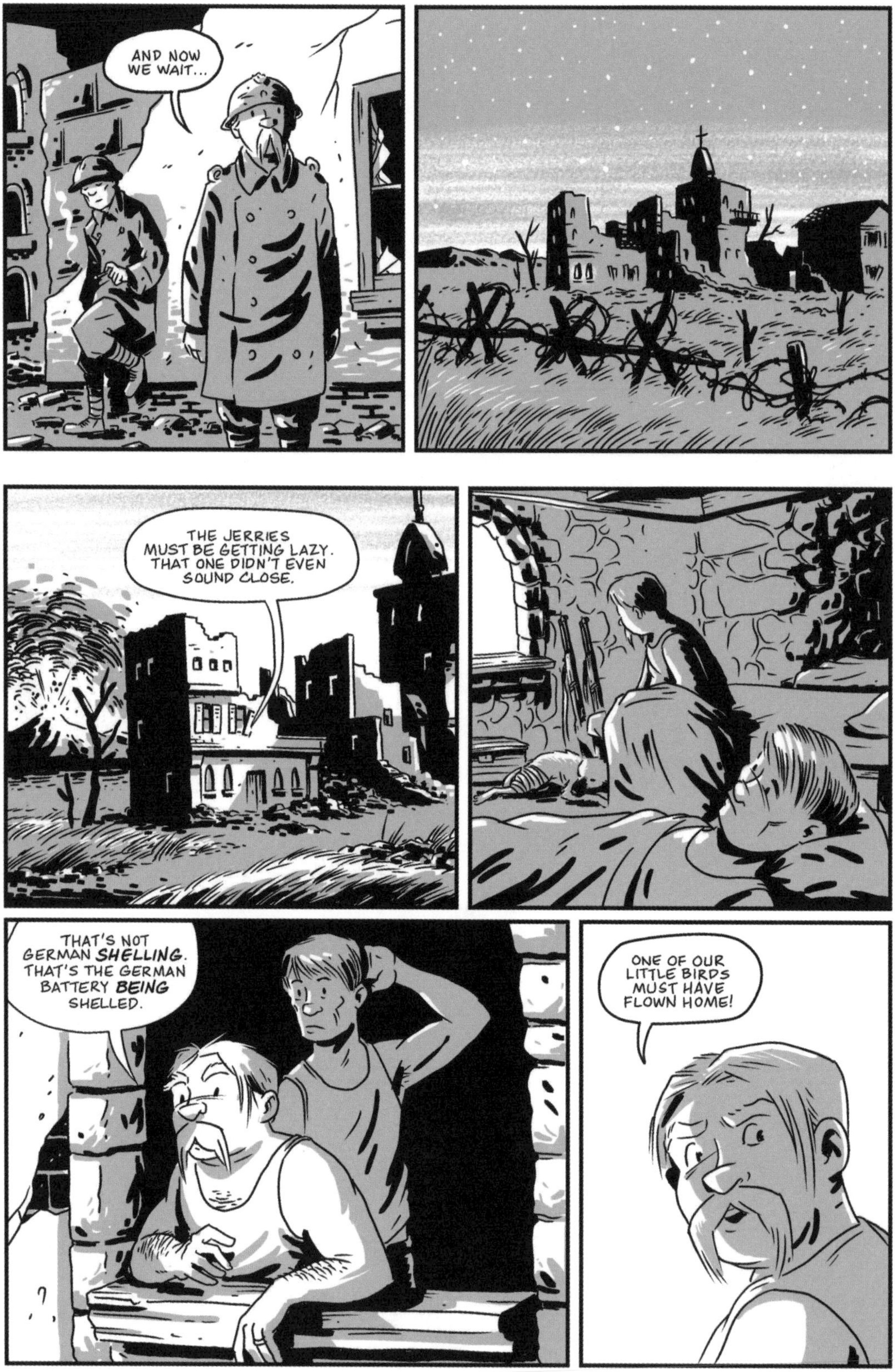
AND NOW WE WAIT...
THE JERRIES MUST BE GETTING LAZY. THAT ONE DIDN'T EVEN SOUND CLOSE.
THAT'S NOT GERMAN **SHELLING**. THAT'S THE GERMAN BATTERY **BEING** SHELLED.
ONE OF OUR LITTLE BIRDS MUST HAVE FLOWN HOME!

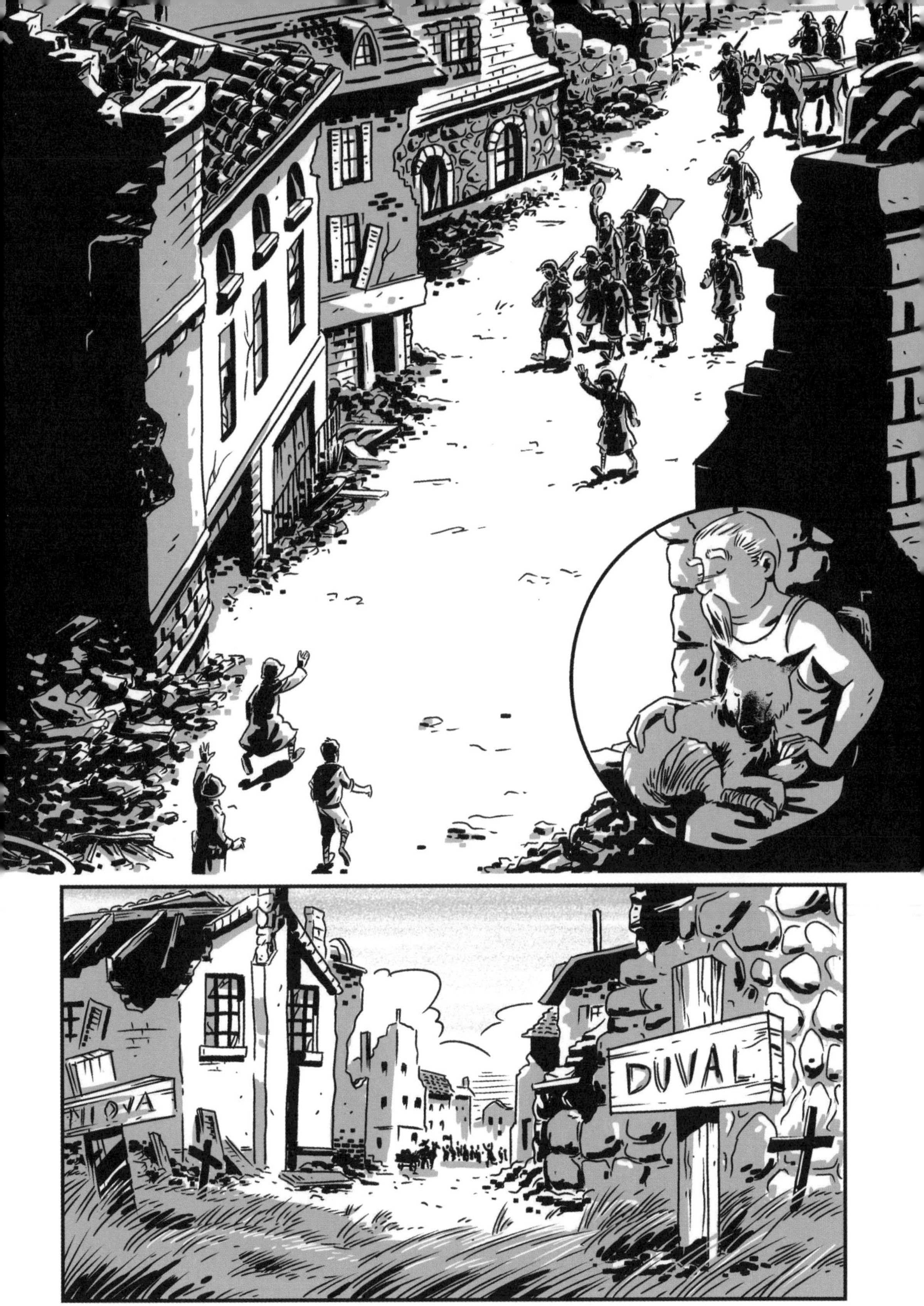
DUVAL

SEAGULLS

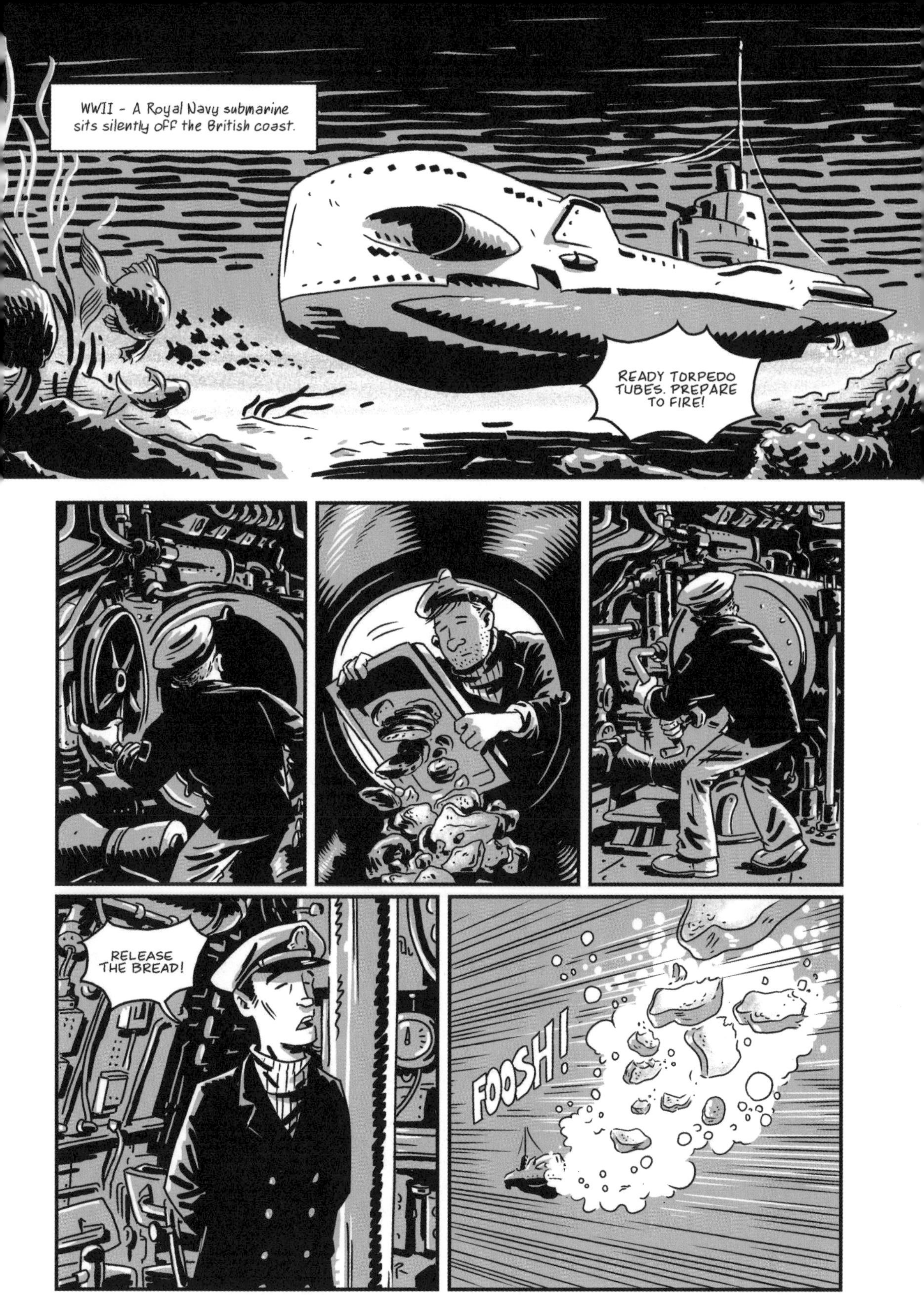

WWII - A Royal Navy submarine sits silently off the British coast.
READY TORPEDO TUBES. PREPARE TO FIRE!
RELEASE THE BREAD!
FOOSH!

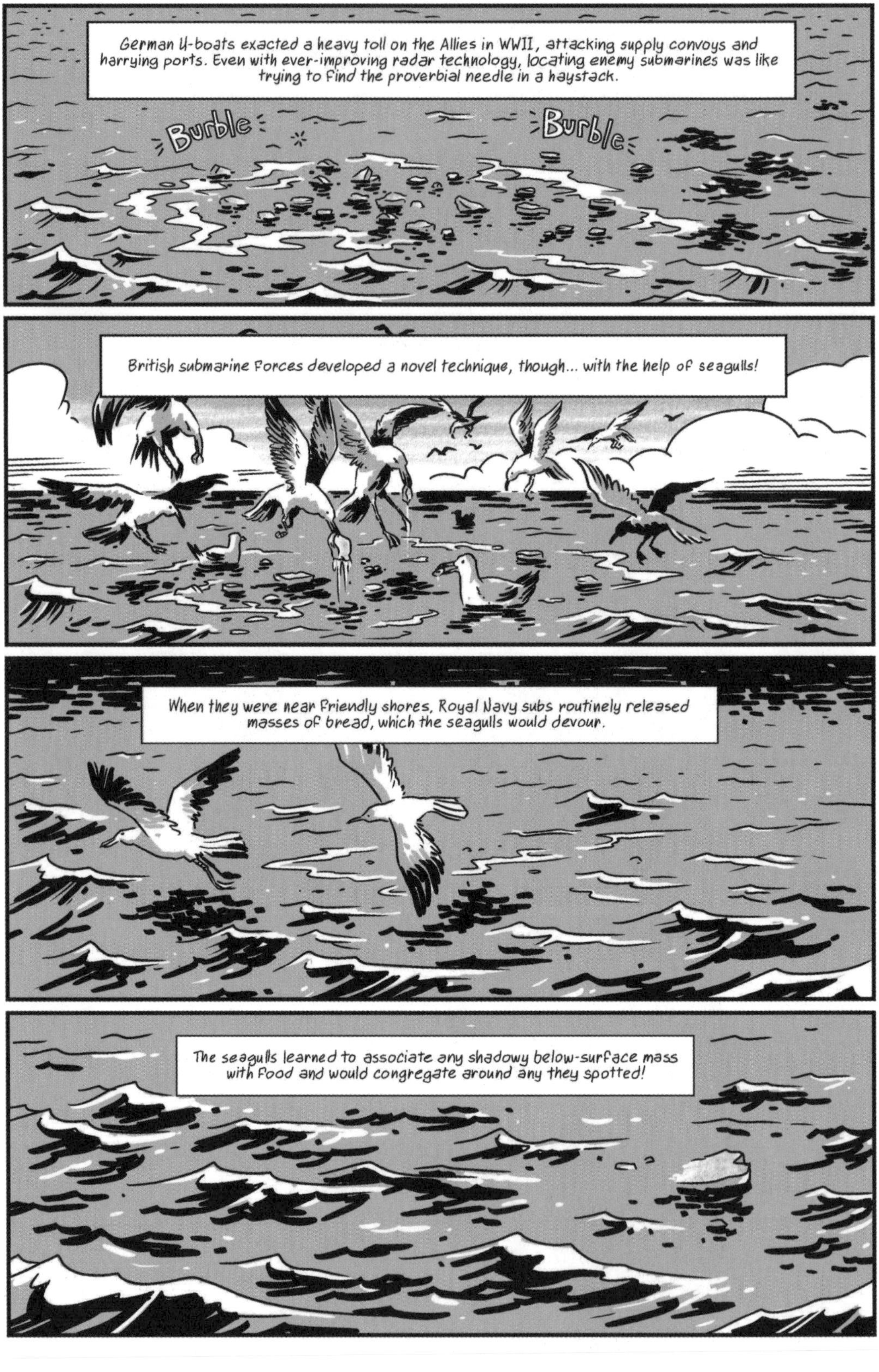
German U-boats exacted a heavy toll on the Allies in WWII, attacking supply convoys and harrying ports. Even with ever-improving radar technology, locating enemy submarines was like trying to find the proverbial needle in a haystack.
Burble
Burble
British submarine forces developed a novel technique, though... with the help of seagulls!
When they were near friendly shores, Royal Navy subs routinely released masses of bread, which the seagulls would devour.
The seagulls learned to associate any shadowy below-surface mass with food and would congregate around any they spotted!

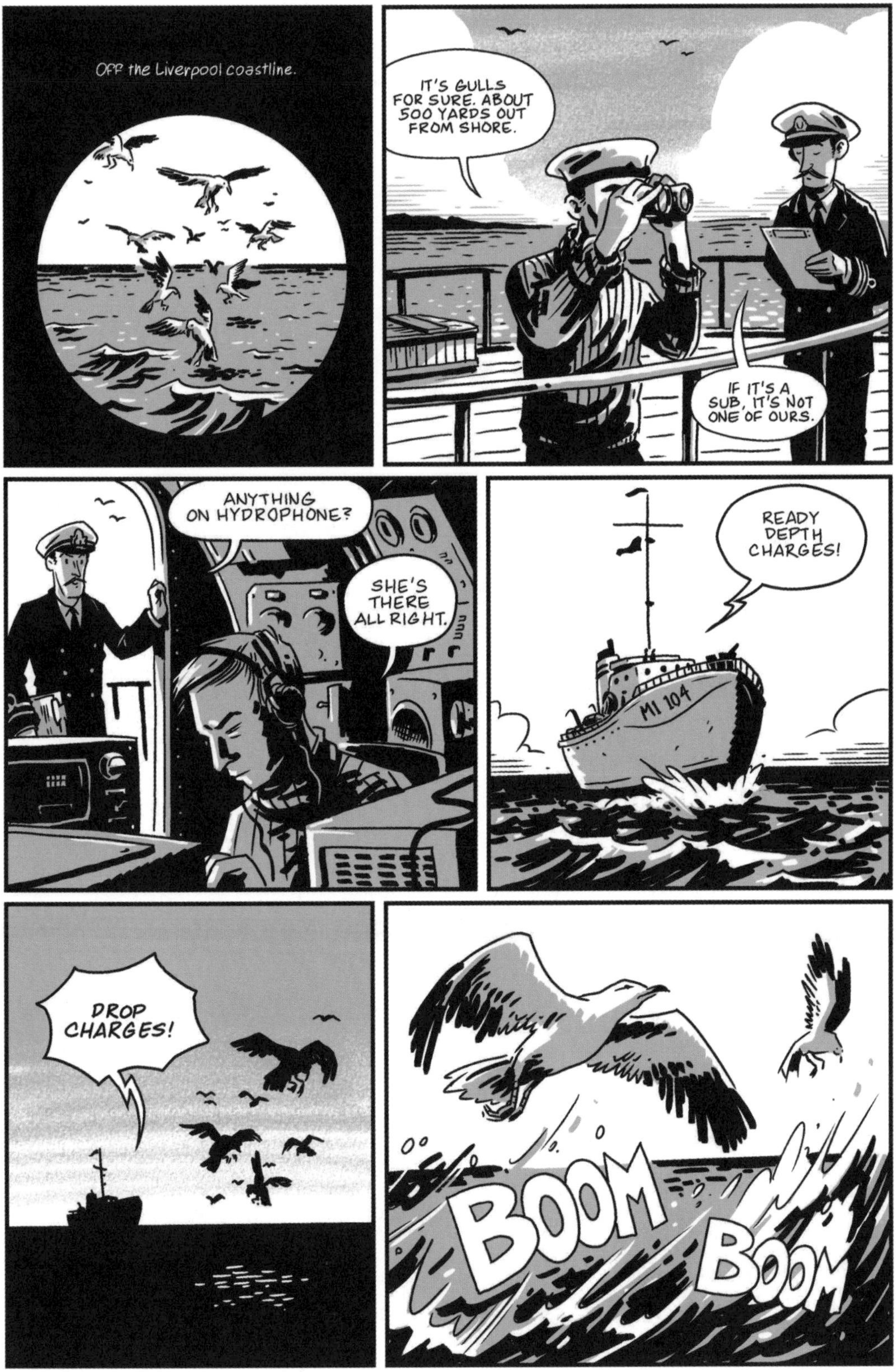
Off the Liverpool coastline.
IT'S GULLS FOR SURE. ABOUT 500 YARDS OUT FROM SHORE.
IF IT'S A SUB, IT'S NOT ONE OF OURS.
ANYTHING ON HYDROPHONE?
SHE'S THERE ALL RIGHT.
READY DEPTH CHARGES!
MI 104
DROP CHARGES!
BOOM
BOOM

MINE-DETECTING
RATS

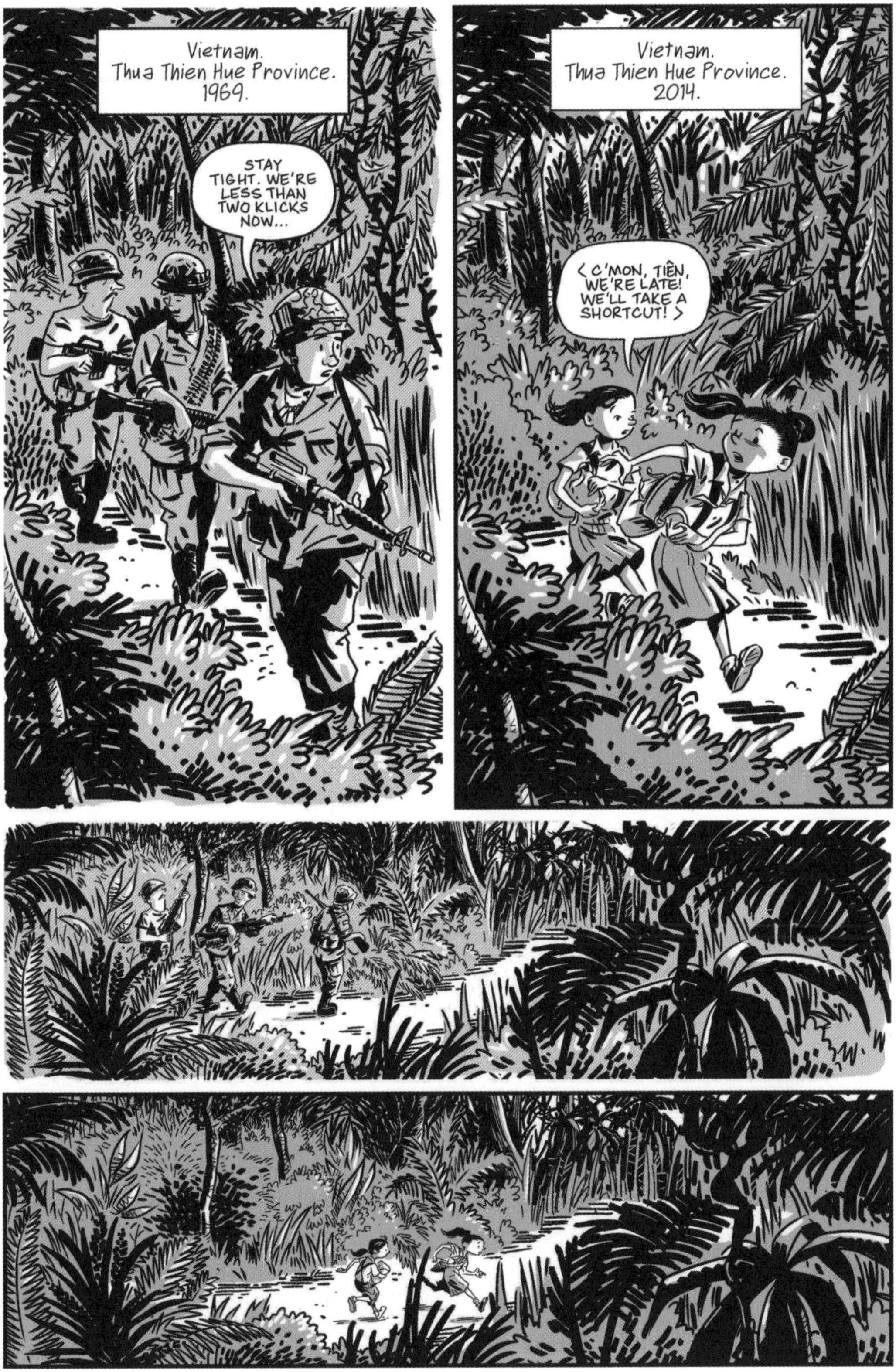
Vietnam.
Thua Thien Hue Province.
1969.
STAY TIGHT. WE'RE LESS THAN TWO KLICKS NOW...
Vietnam.
Thua Thien Hue Province.
2014.
< C'MON, TIÊN, WE'RE LATE! WE'LL TAKE A SHORTCUT! >

HUFF
HUFF
HUFF

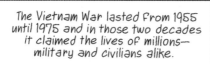
The Vietnam War lasted from 1955 until 1975 and in those two decades it claimed the lives of millions—military and civilians alike.

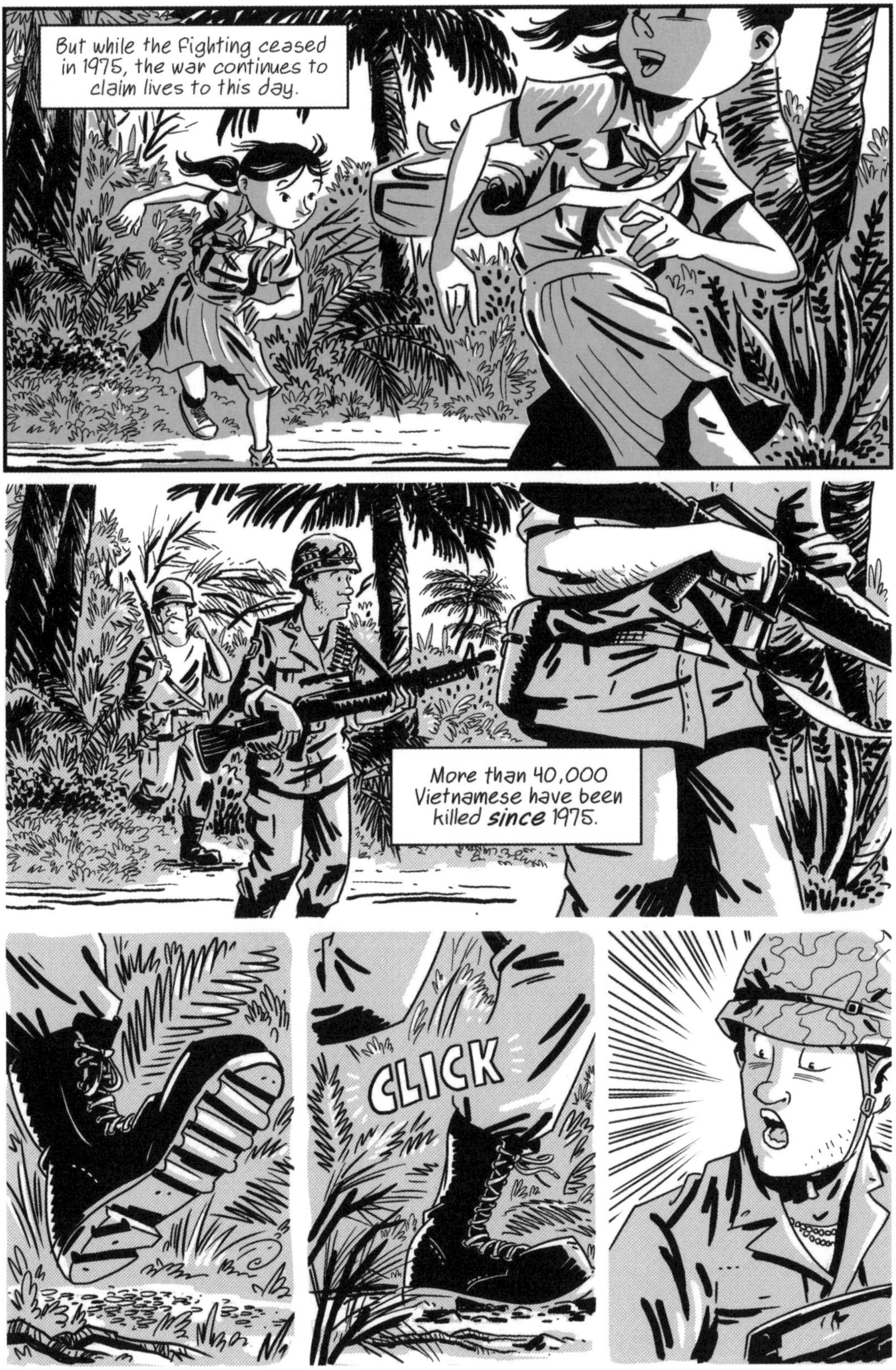
But while the fighting ceased in 1975, the war continues to claim lives to this day.
More than 40,000 Vietnamese have been killed *since* 1975.
CLICK

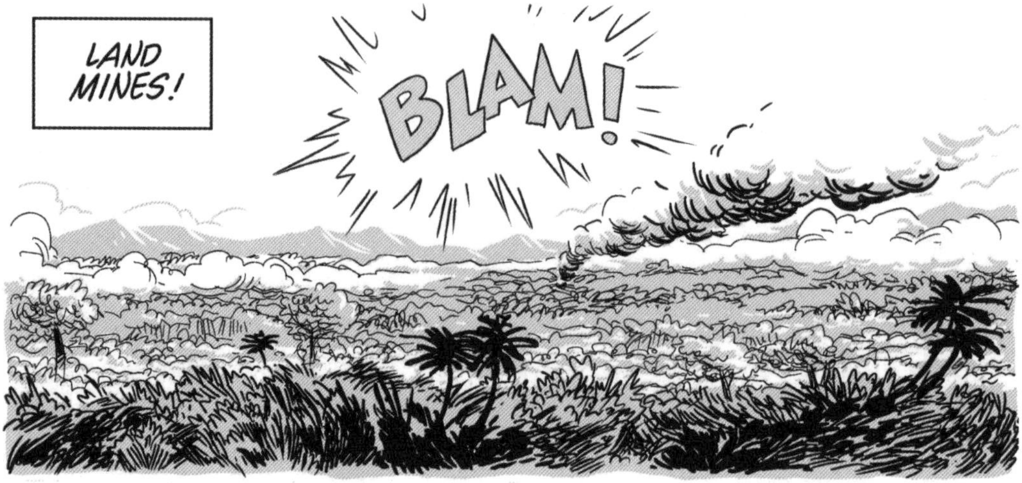
LAND MINES!
BLAM!

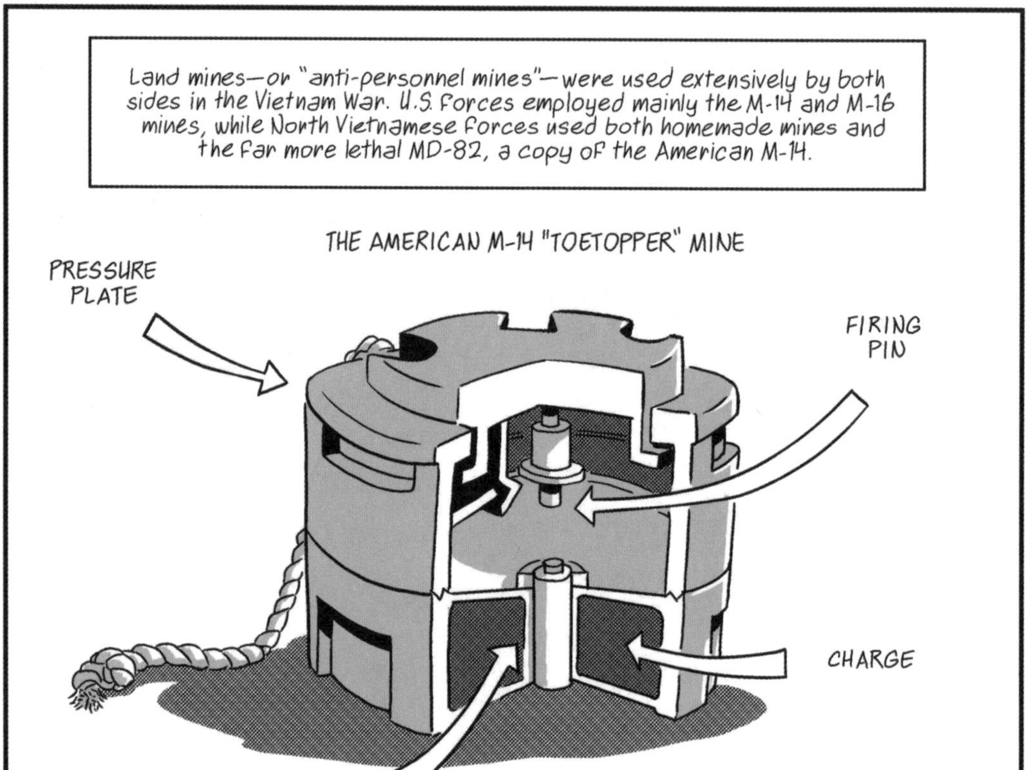
Land mines—or "anti-personnel mines"—were used extensively by both sides in the Vietnam War. U.S. forces employed mainly the M-14 and M-16 mines, while North Vietnamese forces used both homemade mines and the far more lethal MD-82, a copy of the American M-14.
THE AMERICAN M-14 "TOETOPPER" MINE
PRESSURE PLATE
FIRING PIN
CHARGE
DETONATOR
Whatever the variety, all land mines work basically the same way: they're buried in the ground and detonated by pressure when walked over. They cannot be remotely deactivated and often remain "live" and lethal for decades.

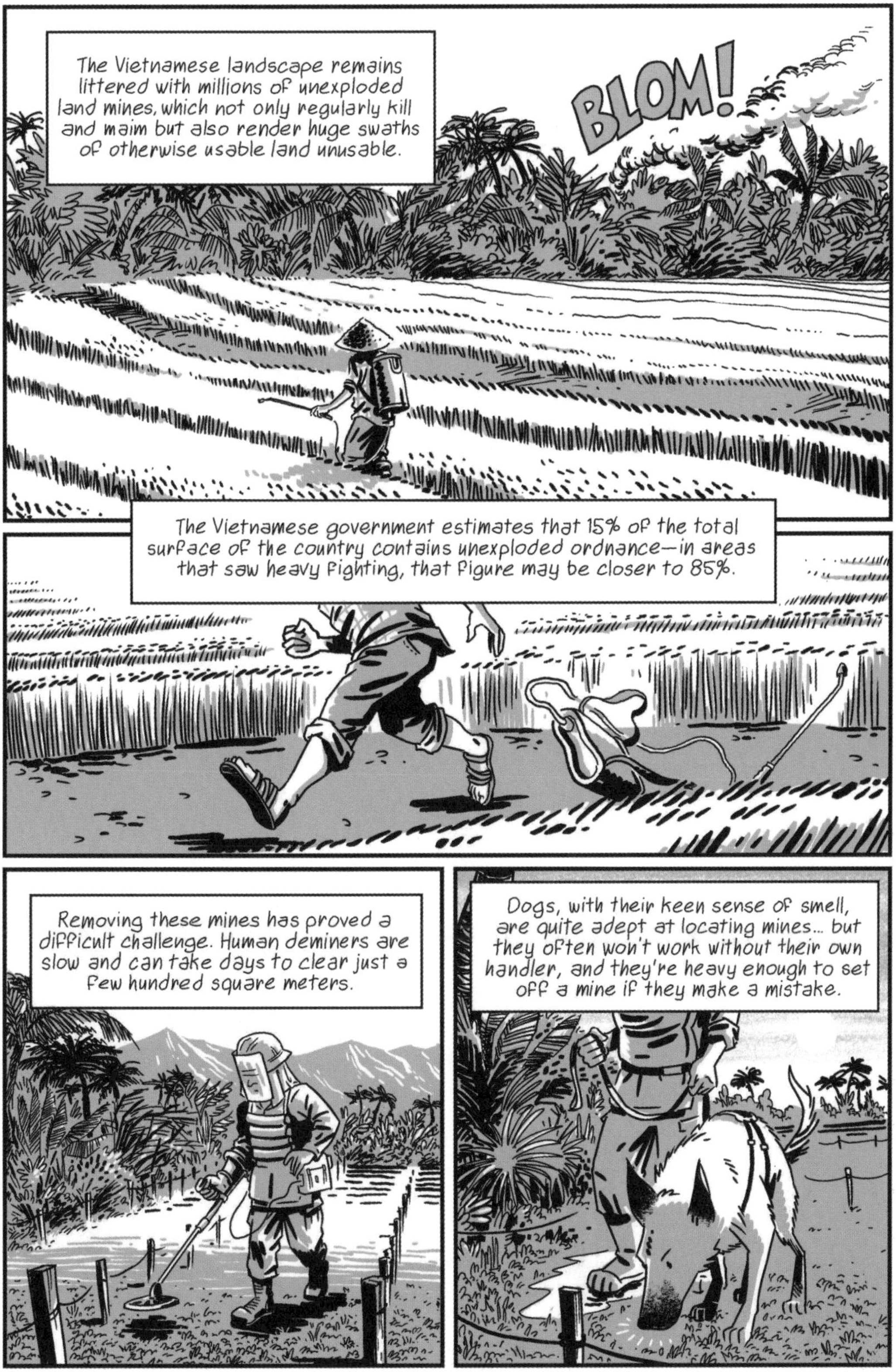

The Vietnamese landscape remains littered with millions of unexploded land mines, which not only regularly kill and maim but also render huge swaths of otherwise usable land unusable.
BLOM!
The Vietnamese government estimates that 15% of the total surface of the country contains unexploded ordnance—in areas that saw heavy fighting, that figure may be closer to 85%.
Removing these mines has proved a difficult challenge. Human deminers are slow and can take days to clear just a few hundred square meters.
Dogs, with their keen sense of smell, are quite adept at locating mines... but they often won't work without their own handler, and they're heavy enough to set off a mine if they make a mistake.

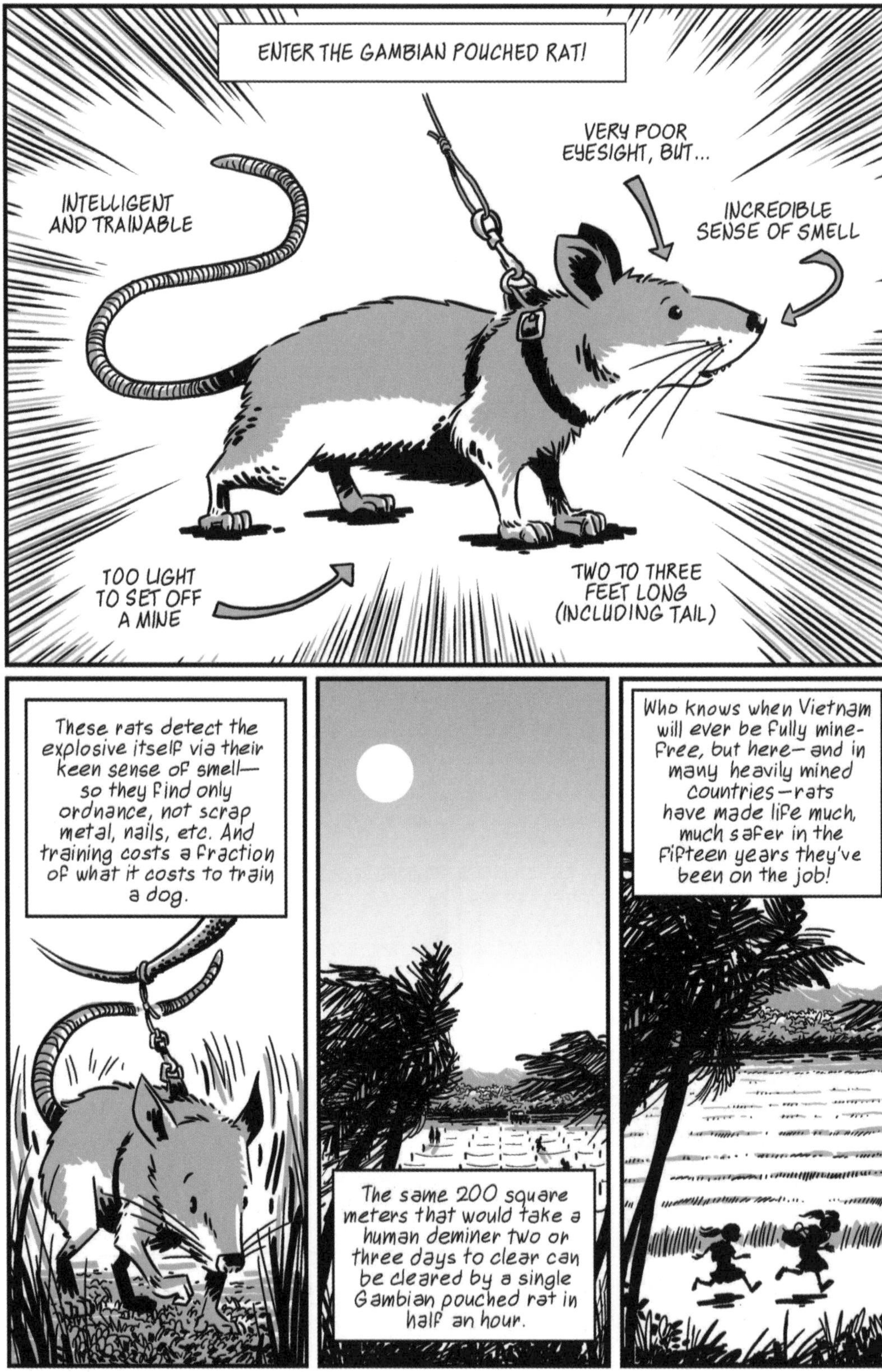
ENTER THE GAMBIAN POUCHED RAT!
INTELLIGENT AND TRAINABLE
VERY POOR EYESIGHT, BUT...
INCREDIBLE SENSE OF SMELL
TOO LIGHT TO SET OFF A MINE
TWO TO THREE FEET LONG (INCLUDING TAIL)
These rats detect the explosive itself via their keen sense of smell— so they find only ordnance, not scrap metal, nails, etc. And training costs a fraction of what it costs to train a dog.
The same 200 square meters that would take a human deminer two or three days to clear can be cleared by a single Gambian pouched rat in half an hour.
Who knows when Vietnam will ever be fully mine-free, but here— and in many heavily mined countries—rats have made life much, much safer in the fifteen years they've been on the job!

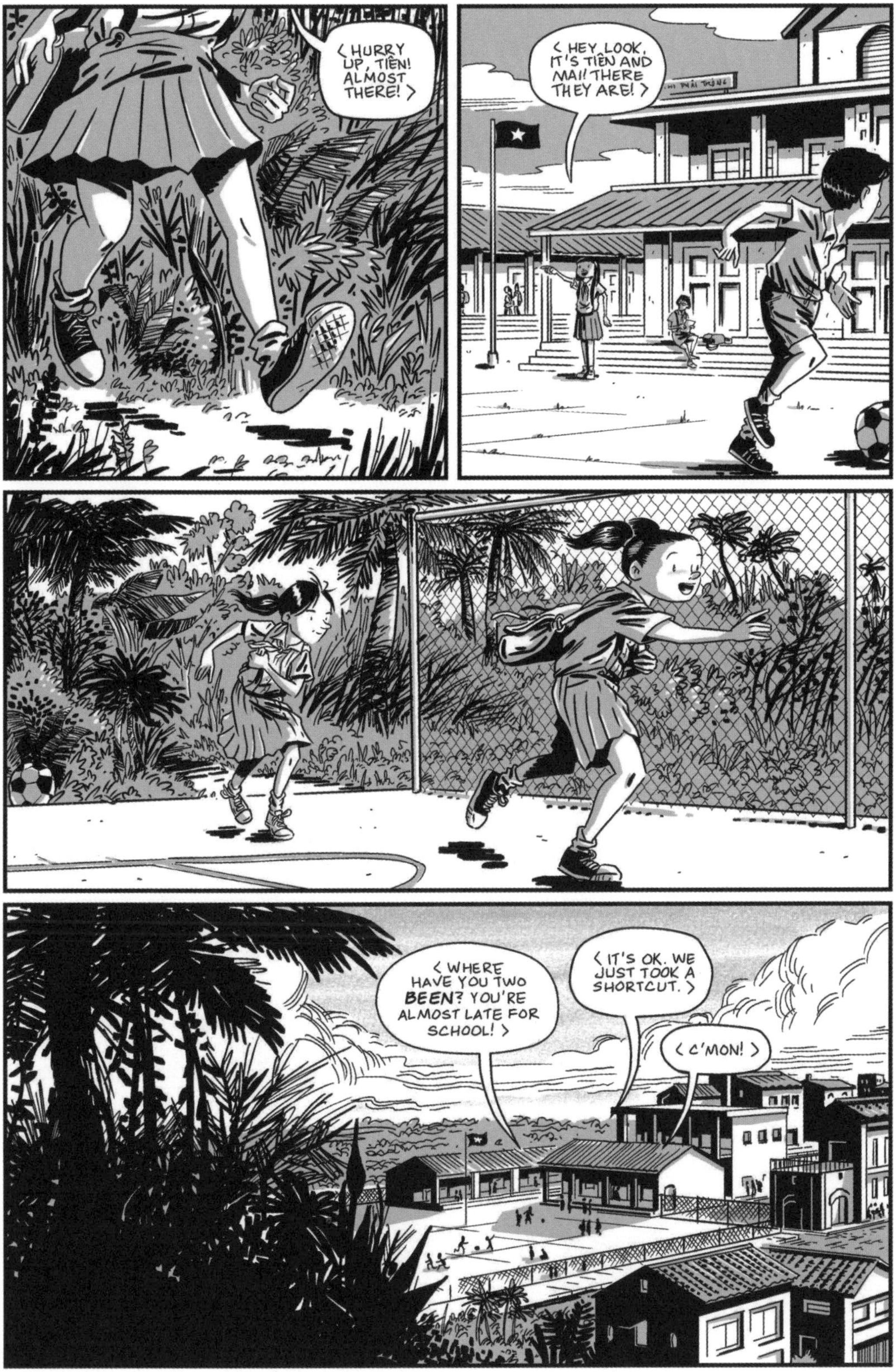
< HURRY UP, TIÊN! ALMOST THERE! >
< HEY LOOK, IT'S TIÊN AND MAI! THERE THEY ARE! >
< WHERE HAVE YOU TWO BEEN? YOU'RE ALMOST LATE FOR SCHOOL! >
< IT'S OK. WE JUST TOOK A SHORTCUT. >
< C'MON! >

WOJTEK

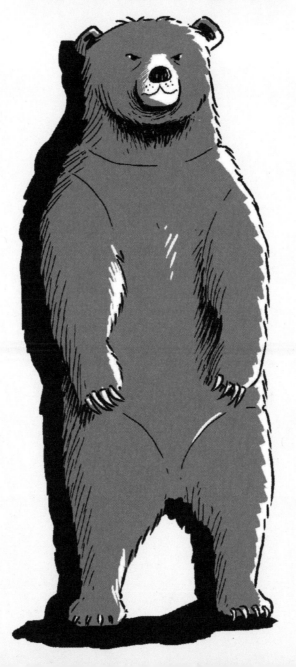

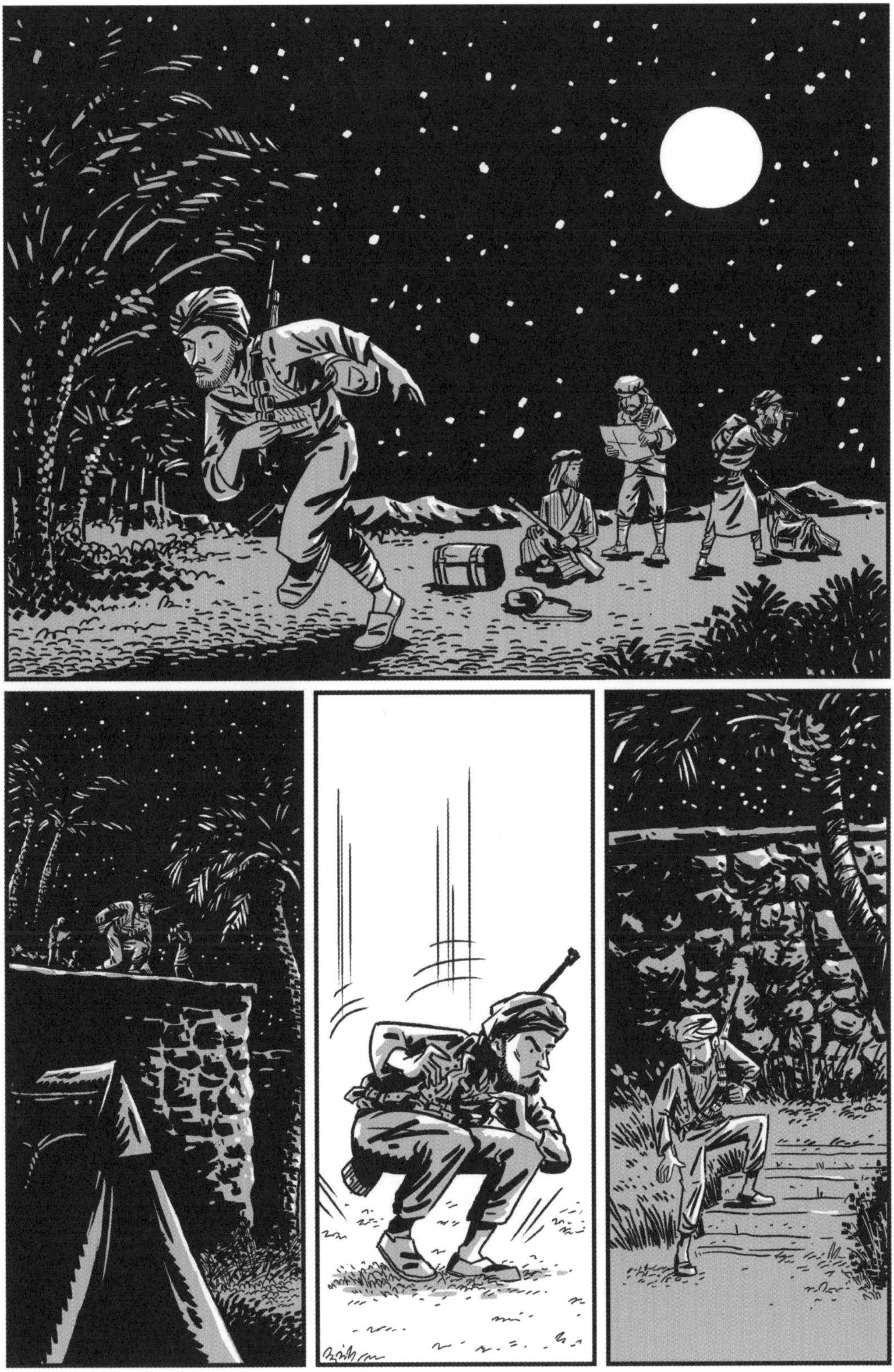

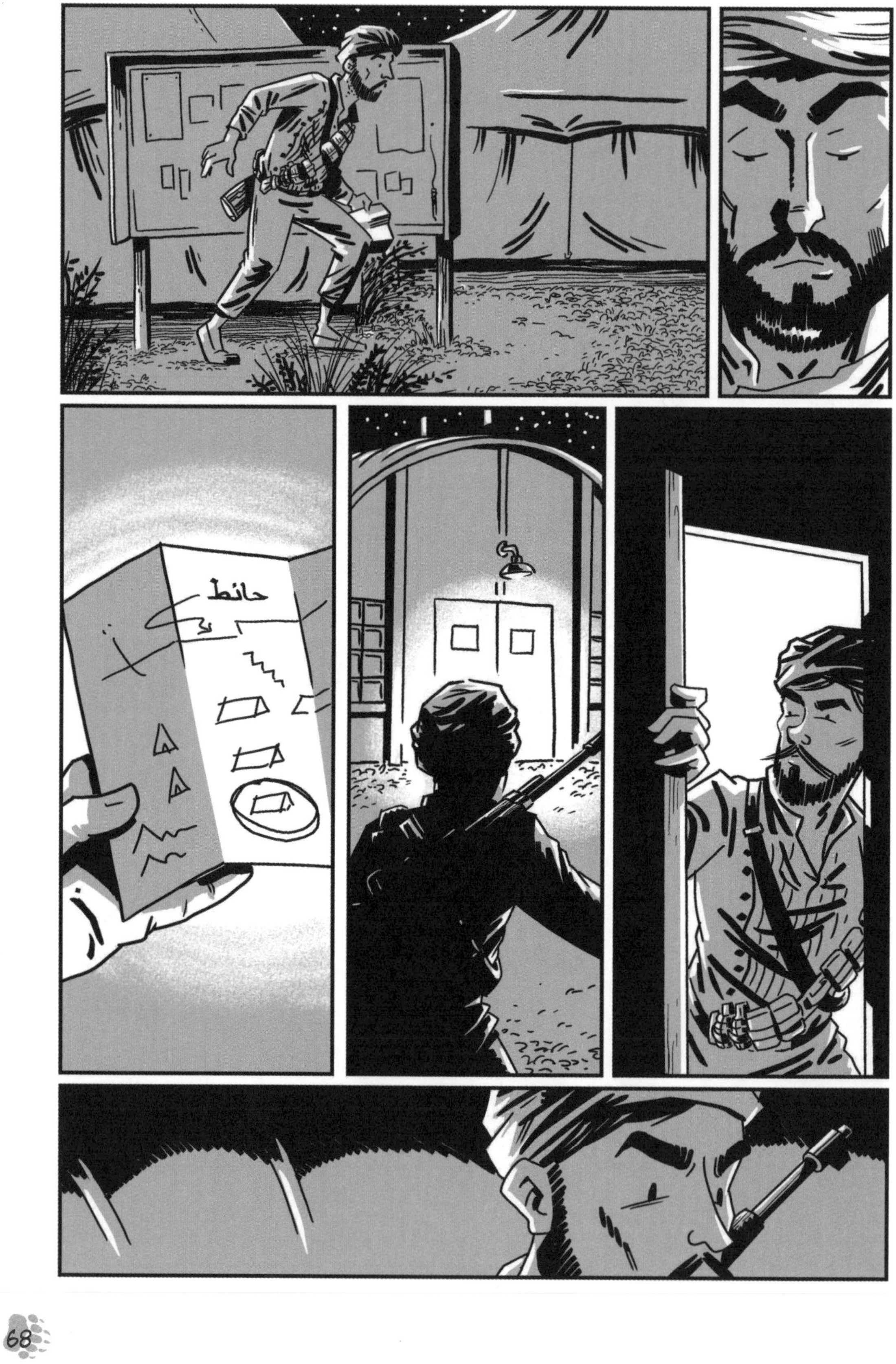
حائط

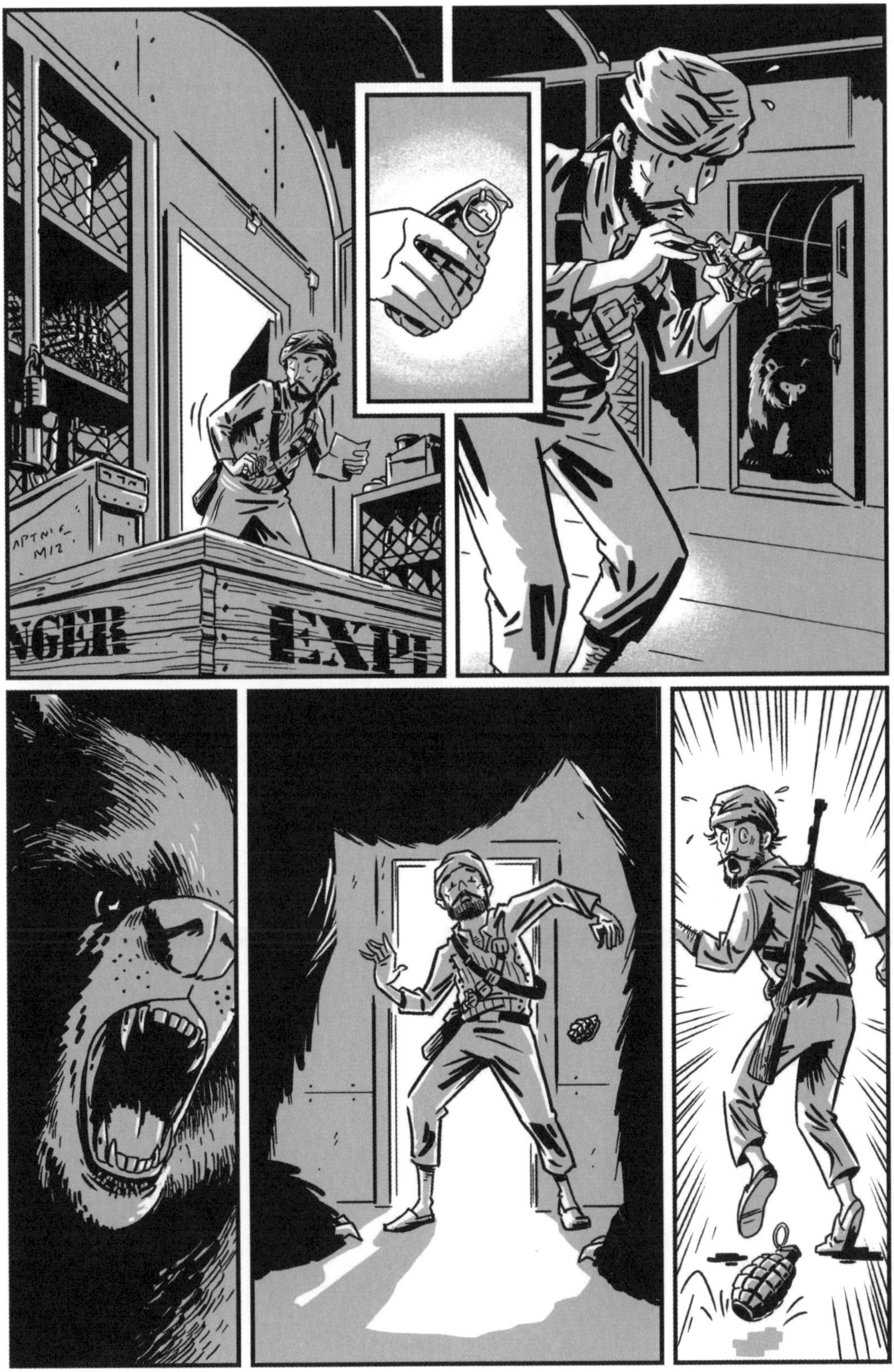
NGER
EXPI

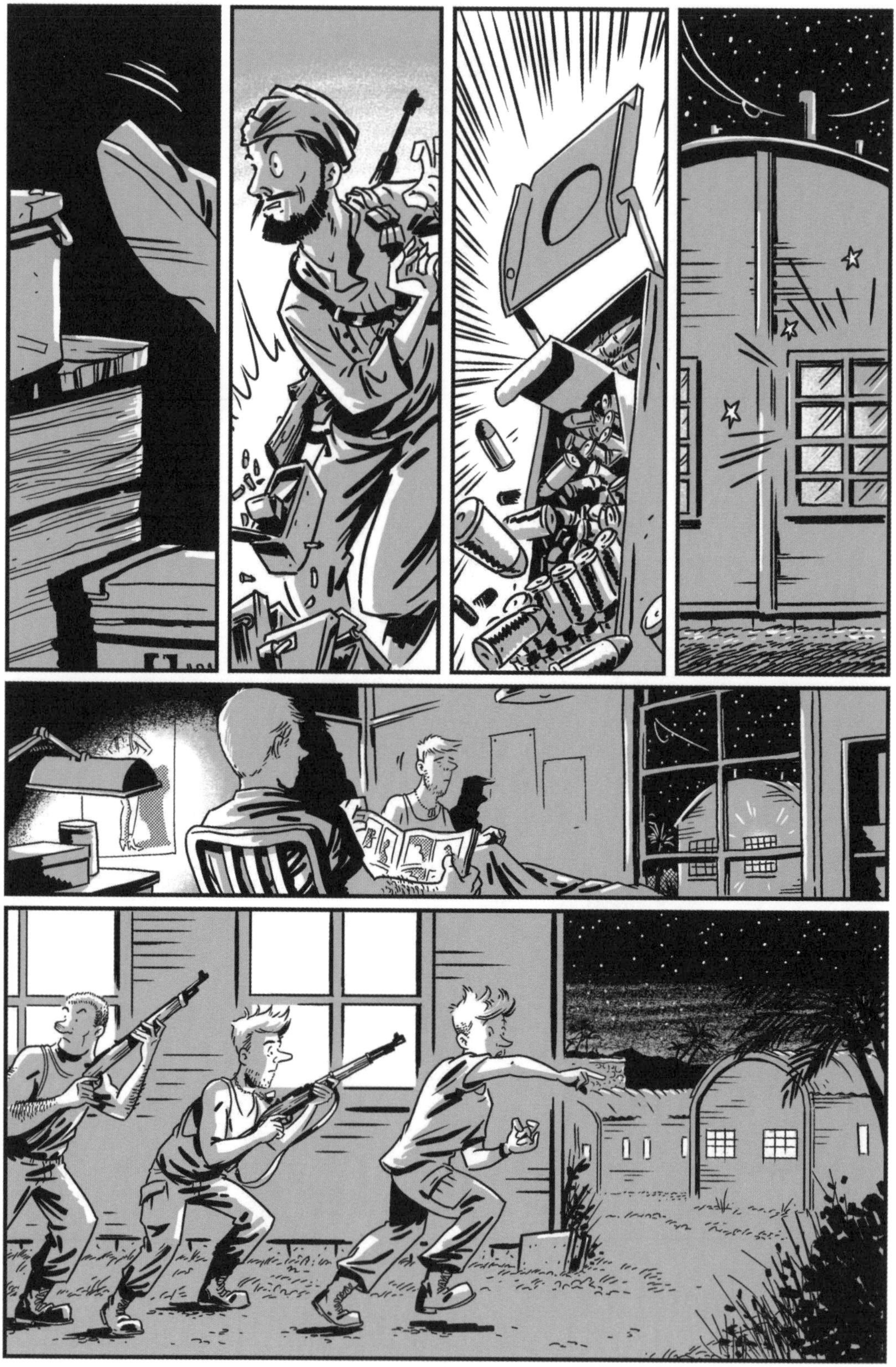

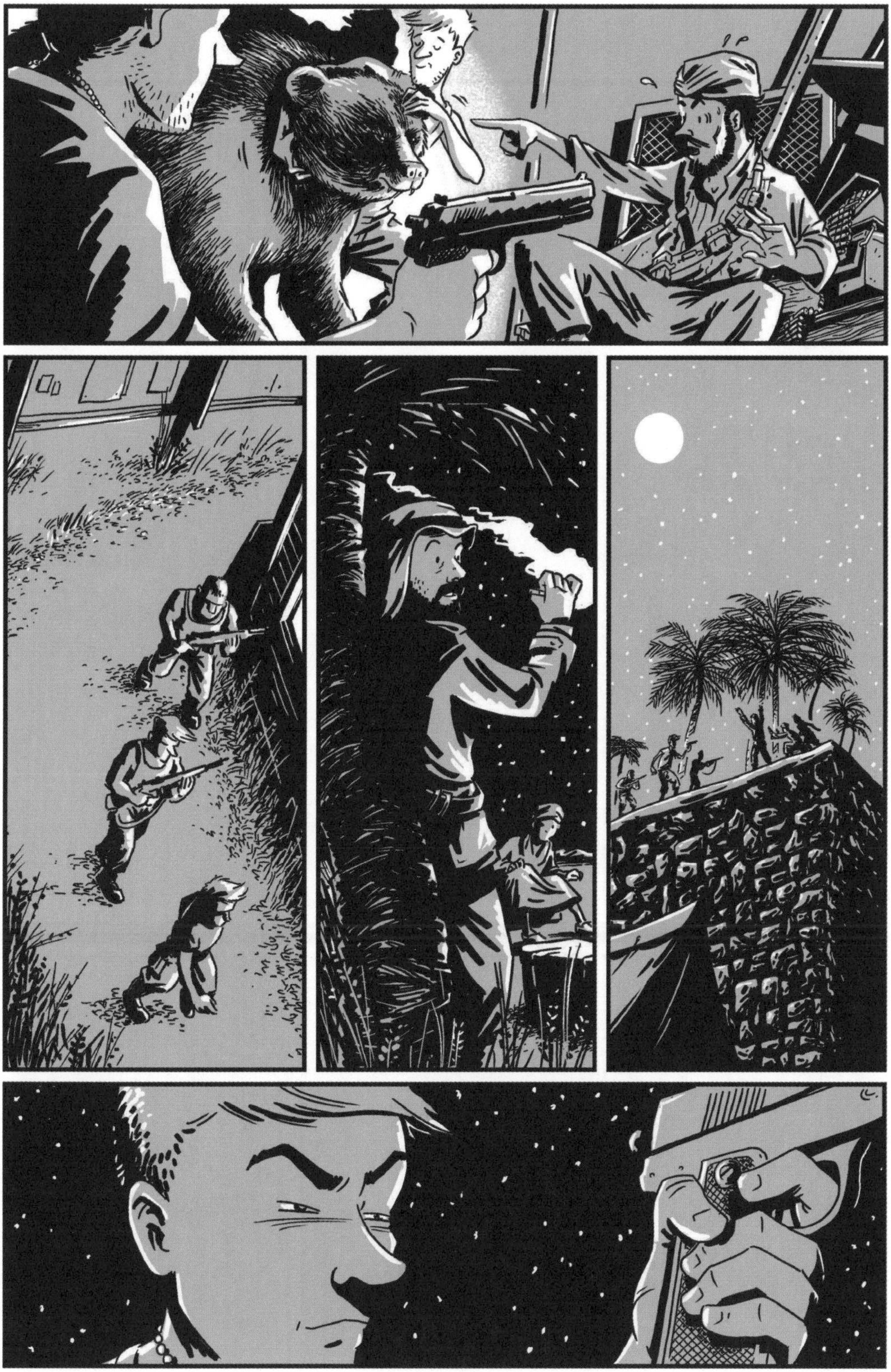

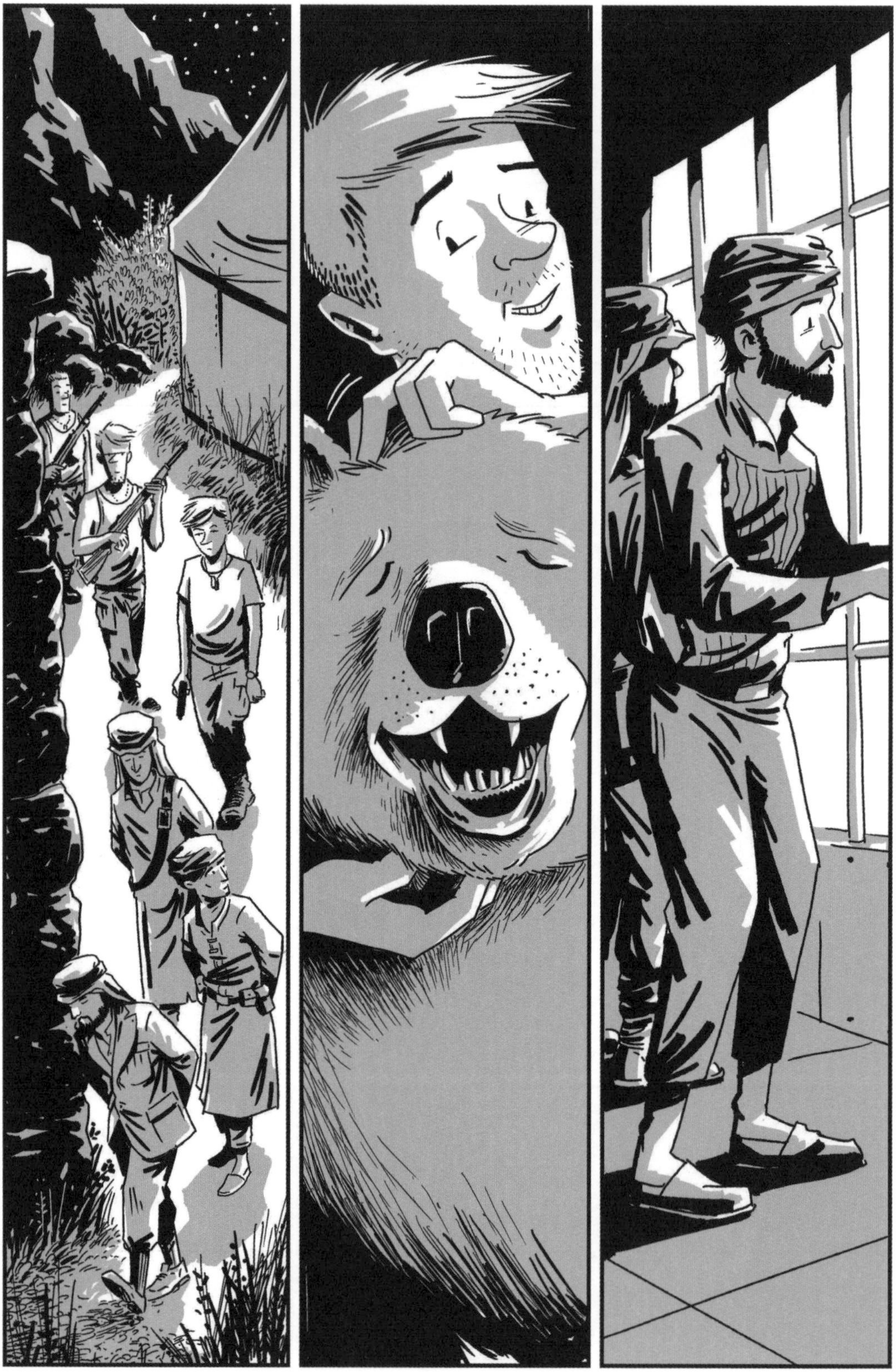

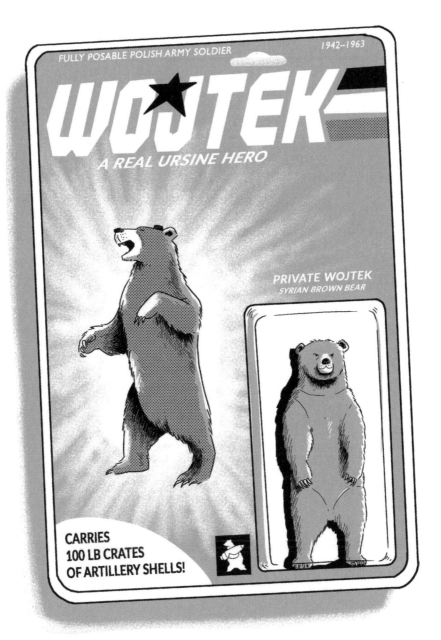

FULLY POSABLE POLISH ARMY SOLDIER   *1942–1963*

WOJTEK

A REAL URSINE HERO

PRIVATE WOJTEK
SYRIAN BROWN BEAR

**CARRIES
100 LB CRATES
OF ARTILLERY SHELLS!**

Wojtek was a Syrian brown bear adopted by a unit of Polish soldiers travelling from the Soviet Union to Iran during WWII. Since regulations forbade mascot animals, Wojtek was given the official rank of private (later corporal) so that he could be listed as an official member of the 22nd Artillery Supply Company.

While living with the Polish soldiers, he adopted many of their habits and was known to enjoy a cup of coffee in the morning, a beer or two in the evening, and even saluted passing officers. Among his best-known exploits were loading 100 lb. crates of artillery shells during the Battle of Monte Cassino... and foiling a planned Iraqi raid by surprising the party's advance scout.

SLUGS

Some of the innovations that have saved thousands of lives in wars are well known...

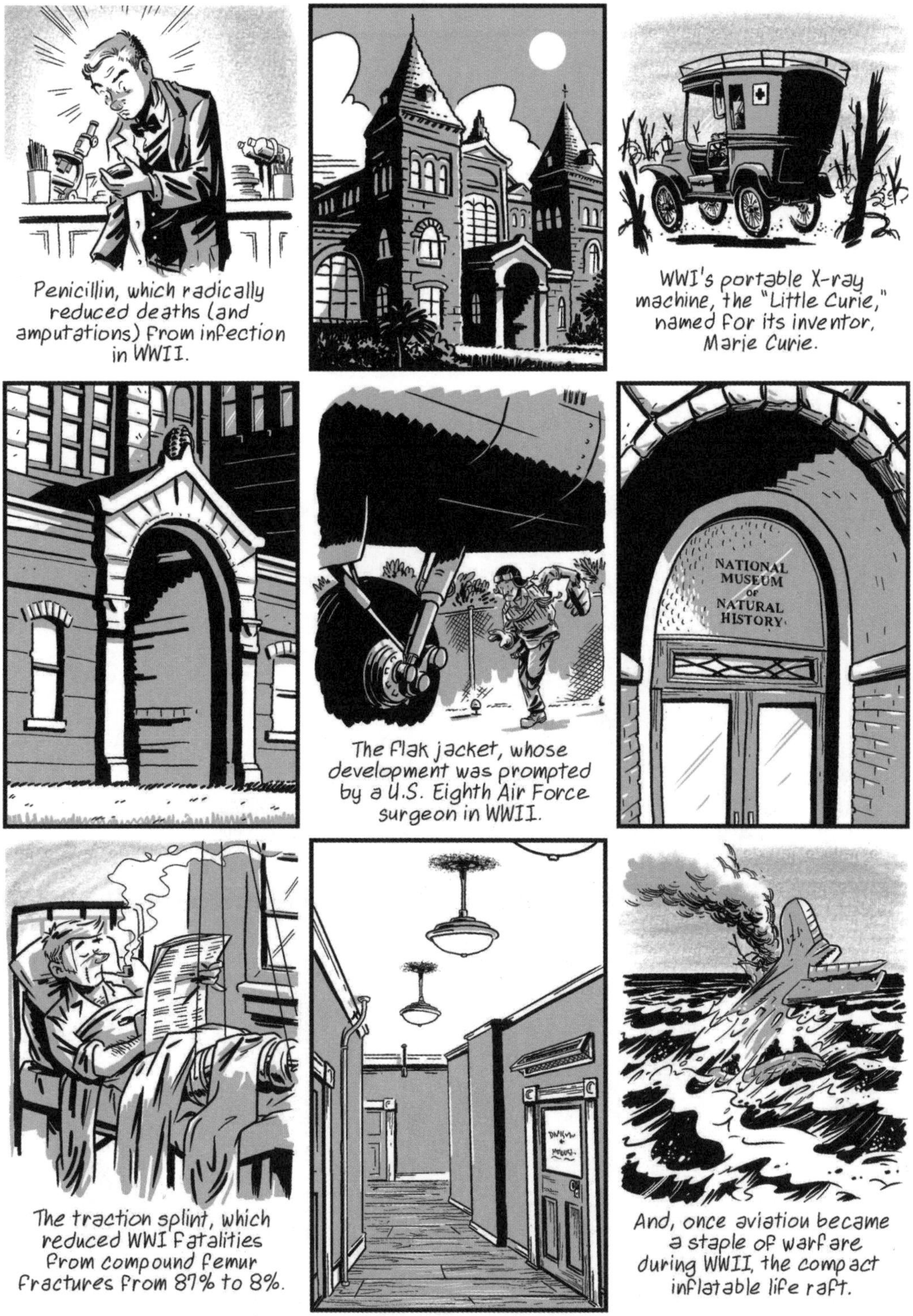
Penicillin, which radically reduced deaths (and amputations) from infection in WWII.
WWI's portable X-ray machine, the "Little Curie," named for its inventor, Marie Curie.
NATIONAL MUSEUM OF NATURAL HISTORY
The flak jacket, whose development was prompted by a U.S. Eighth Air Force surgeon in WWII.
The traction splint, which reduced WWI fatalities from compound femur fractures from 87% to 8%.
And, once aviation became a staple of warfare during WWII, the compact inflatable life raft.

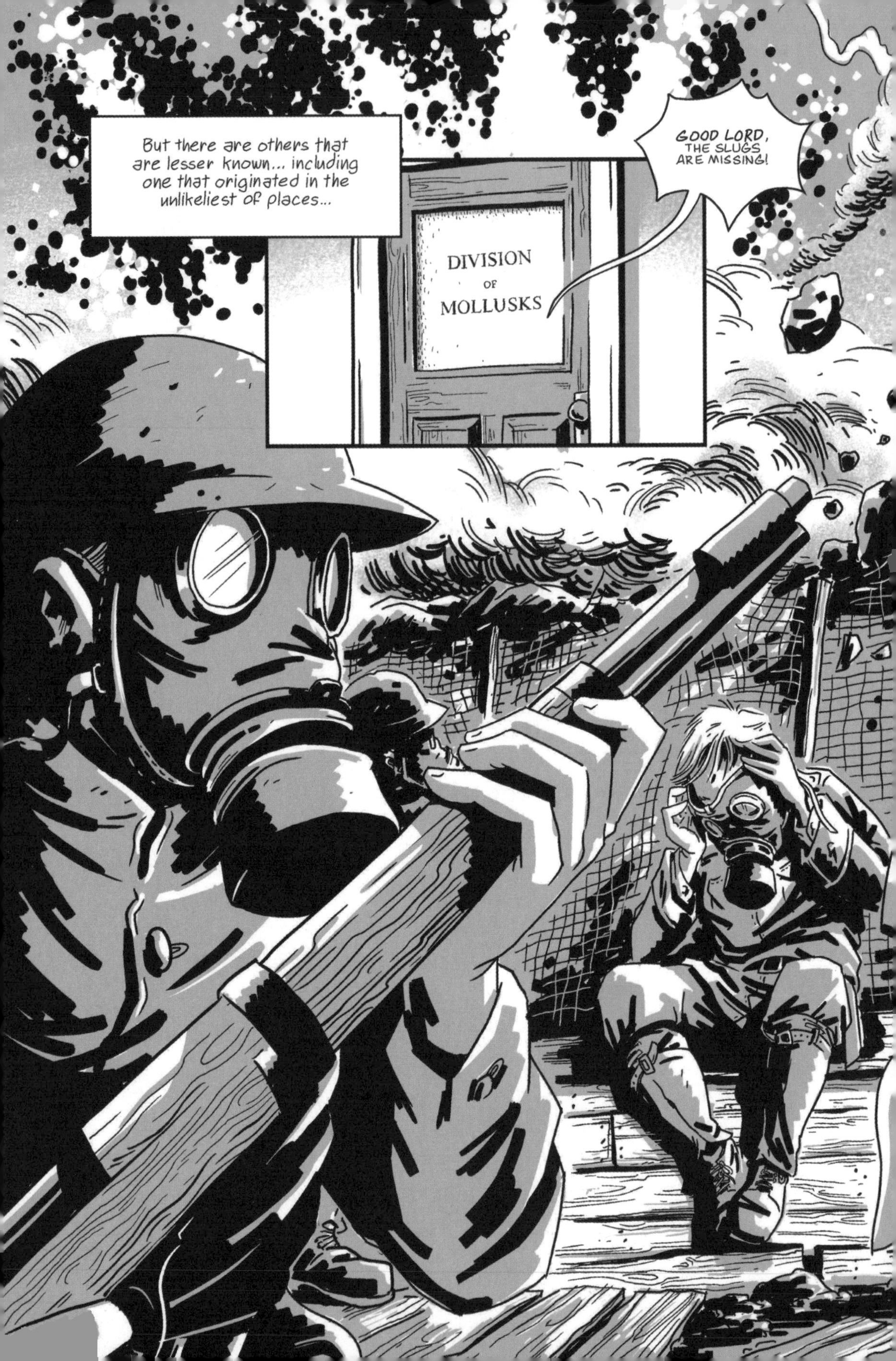
But there are others that are lesser known... including one that originated in the unlikeliest of places...
DIVISION OF MOLLUSKS
GOOD LORD, THE SLUGS ARE MISSING!

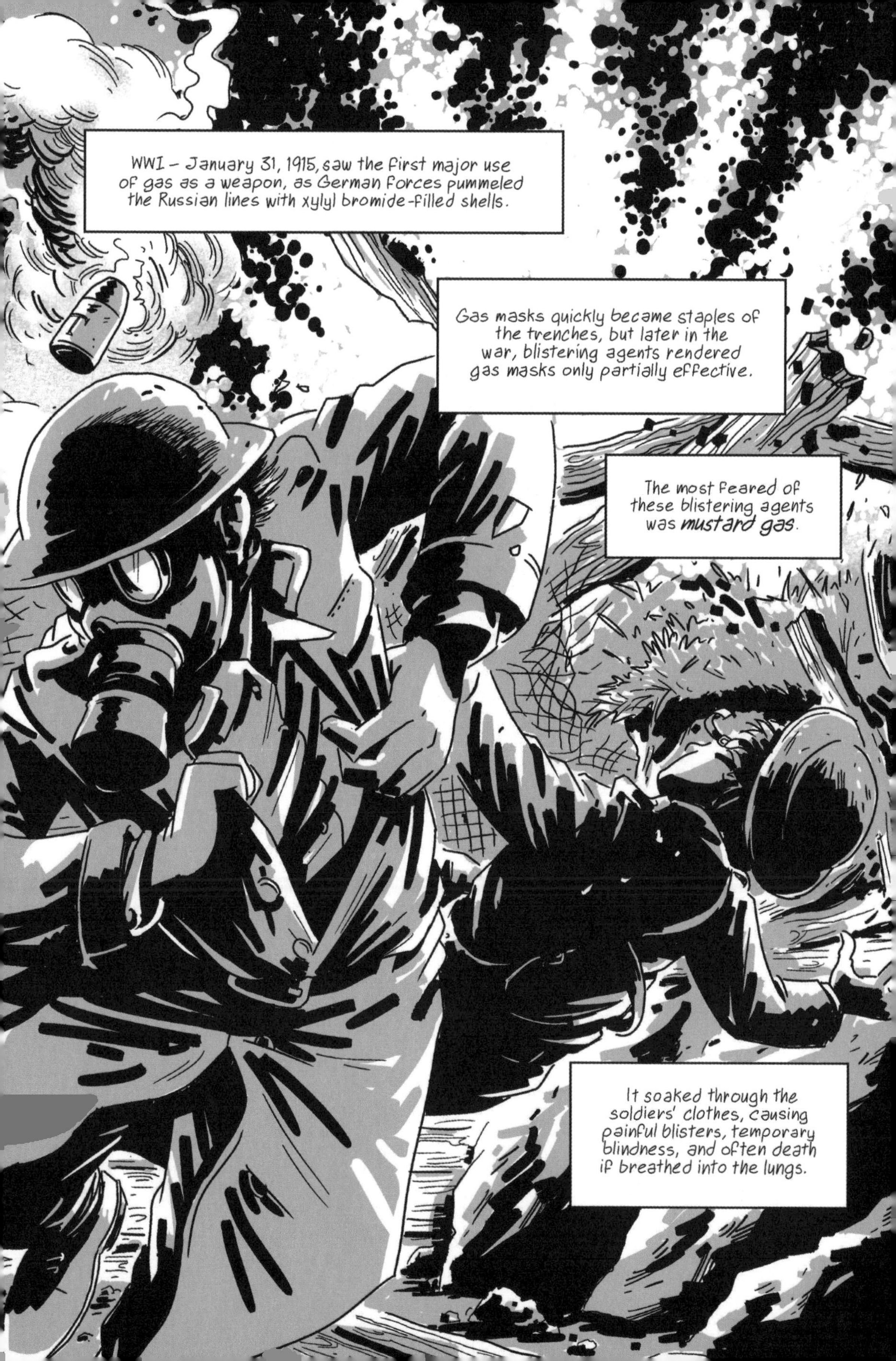
WWI – January 31, 1915, saw the first major use of gas as a weapon, as German forces pummeled the Russian lines with xylyl bromide-filled shells.
Gas masks quickly became staples of the trenches, but later in the war, blistering agents rendered gas masks only partially effective.
The most feared of these blistering agents was *mustard gas*.
It soaked through the soldiers' clothes, causing painful blisters, temporary blindness, and often death if breathed into the lungs.

For years the U.S. Army tried to develop some sort of mustard gas detection system, but it was naturalist Paul Bartsch who would solve the problem.

Bartsch began his career researching mollusks and later served as the assistant curator of the Division of Mollusks at what's now the Smithsonian Institution.

He also studied ornithology and kept a rare Carolina parakeet as a pet— even napping side by side with the bird on occasion.

But it was his insight into *slugs* that would help the war effort.

WHY, **HERE** THEY ARE.

HOW ODD...

While recovering some slugs that had escaped into a furnace room, Bartsch noticed that they were "visibly distressed" by the tiny amount of gas present in the air.

He eventually discovered that slugs could detect airborne mustard gas at one part in 12 million— well below the concentration lethal to humans.

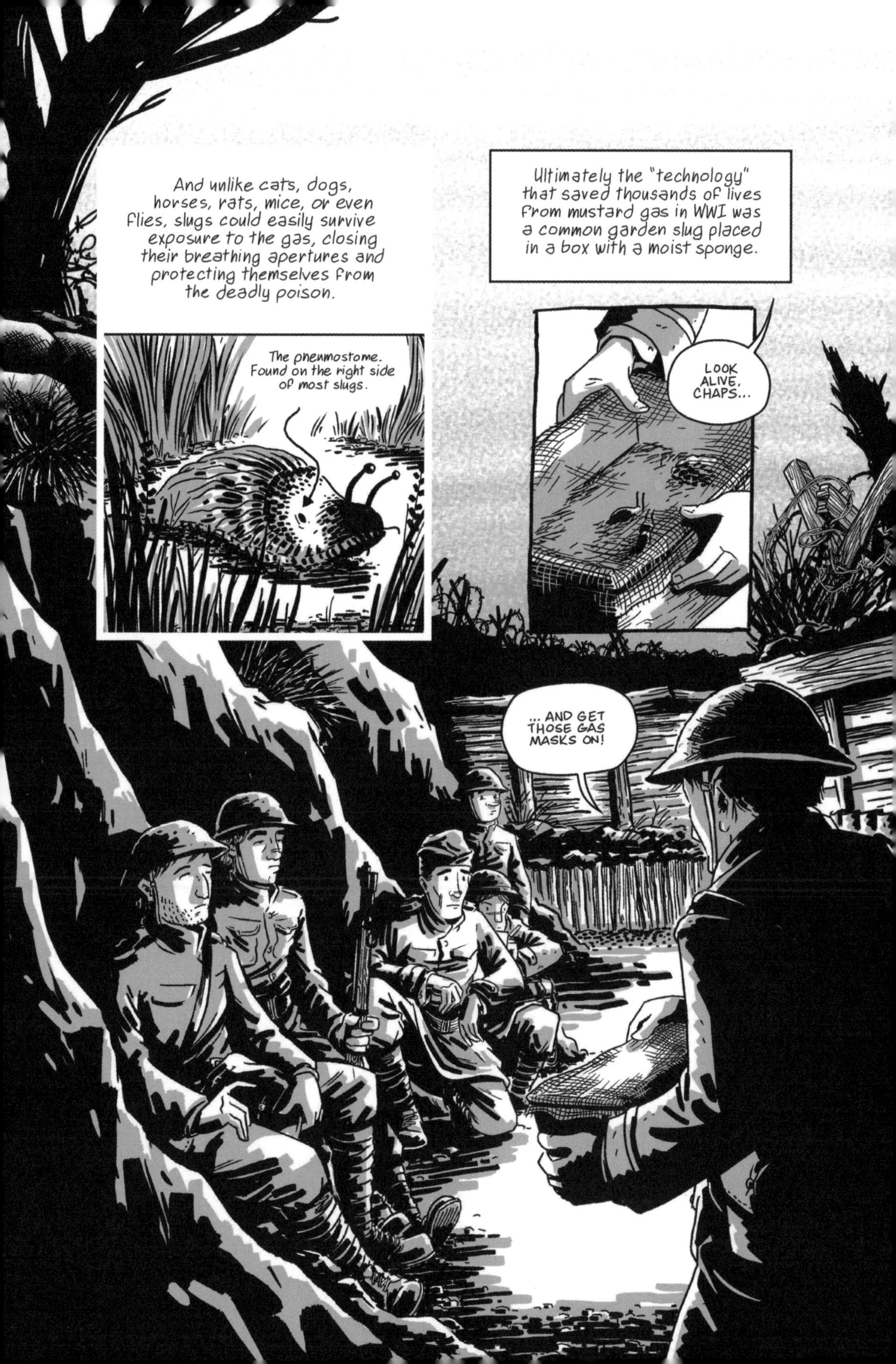
And unlike cats, dogs, horses, rats, mice, or even flies, slugs could easily survive exposure to the gas, closing their breathing apertures and protecting themselves from the deadly poison.
The pneumostome. Found on the right side of most slugs.
Ultimately the "technology" that saved thousands of lives from mustard gas in WWI was a common garden slug placed in a box with a moist sponge.
LOOK ALIVE, CHAPS...
... AND GET THOSE GAS MASKS ON!

HORSES

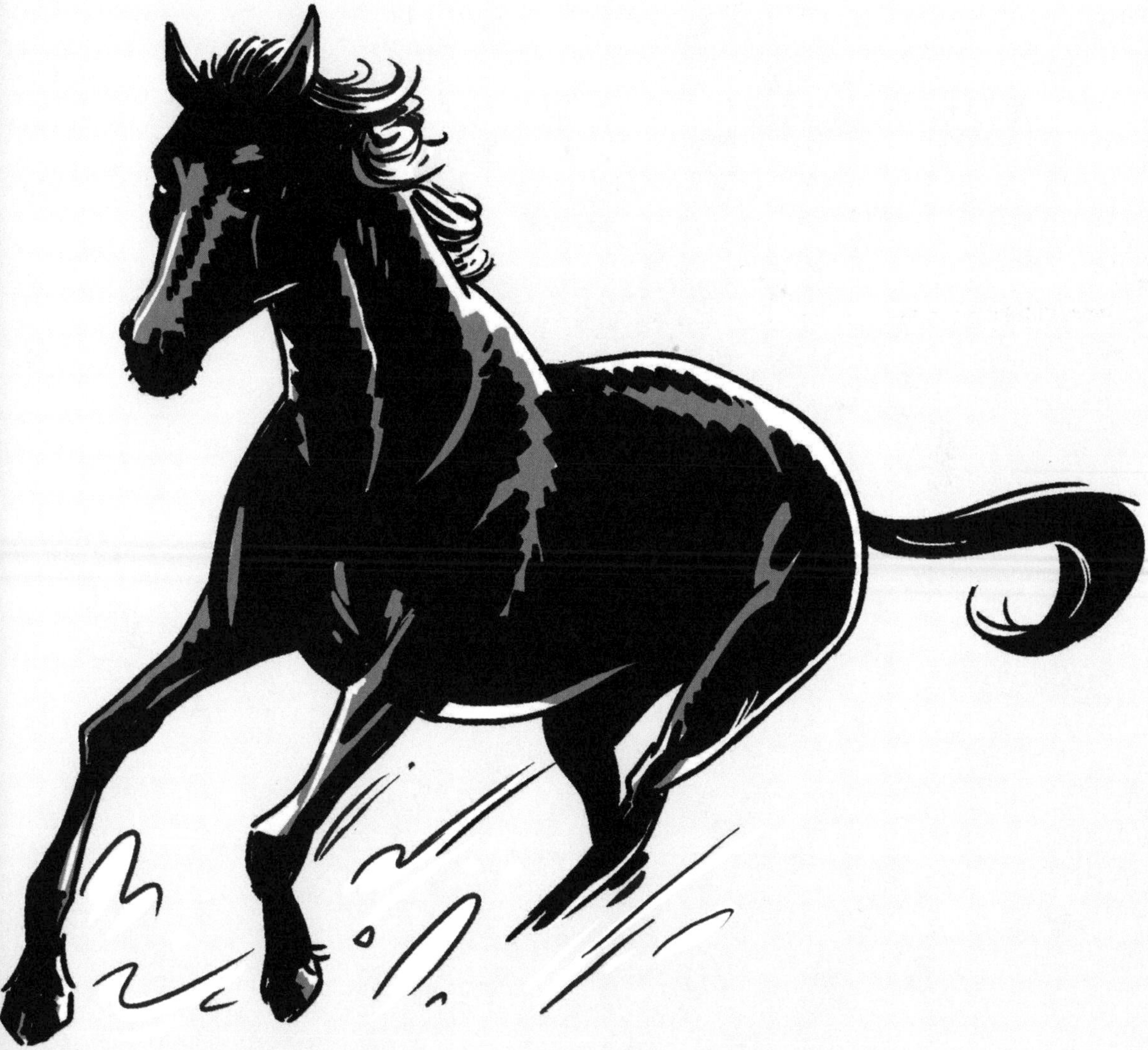

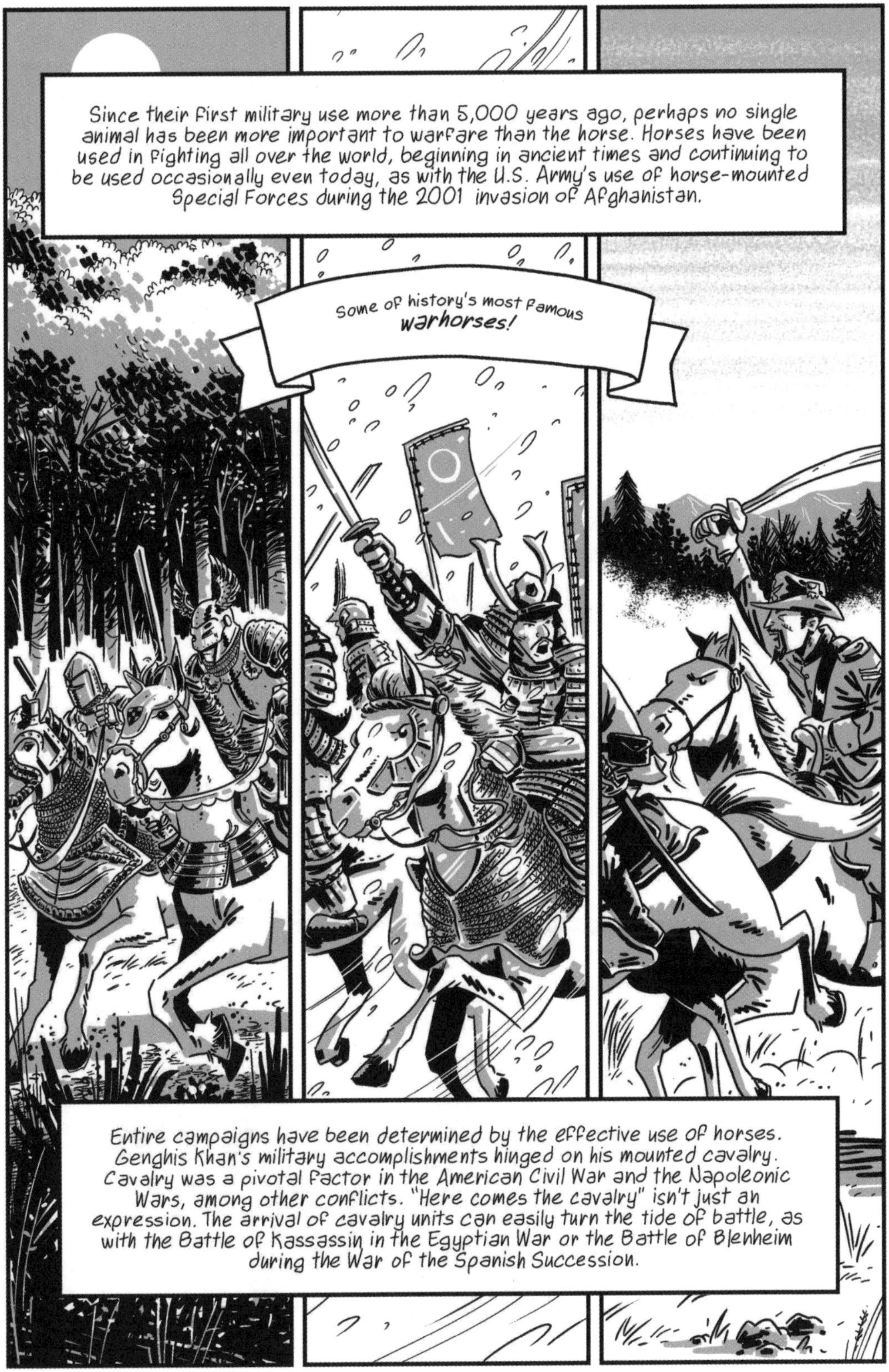
Since their first military use more than 5,000 years ago, perhaps no single animal has been more important to warfare than the horse. Horses have been used in fighting all over the world, beginning in ancient times and continuing to be used occasionally even today, as with the U.S. Army's use of horse-mounted Special Forces during the 2001 invasion of Afghanistan.
Some of history's most famous warhorses!
Entire campaigns have been determined by the effective use of horses. Genghis Khan's military accomplishments hinged on his mounted cavalry. Cavalry was a pivotal factor in the American Civil War and the Napoleonic Wars, among other conflicts. "Here comes the cavalry" isn't just an expression. The arrival of cavalry units can easily turn the tide of battle, as with the Battle of Kassassin in the Egyptian War or the Battle of Blenheim during the War of the Spanish Succession.

Perhaps the most famous military horse of all time is Alexander the Great's horse, Bucephalus. The exact details of Bucephalus' life have become intermixed with legend, but as the steed of one of antiquity's greatest military leaders, he most certainly accompanied Alexander in many of his military campaigns to establish an empire from Greece all the way to India.

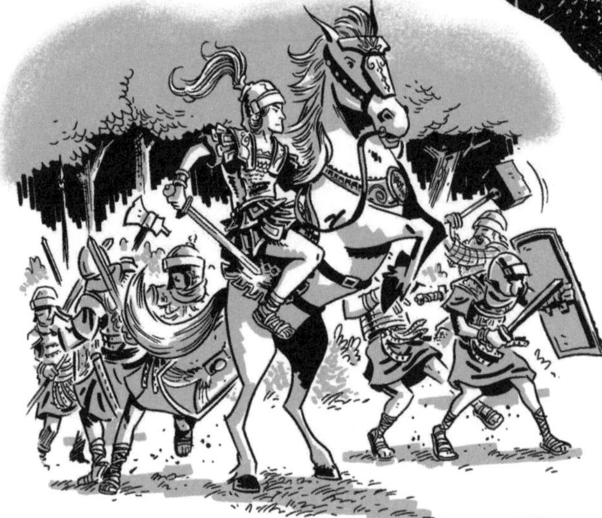

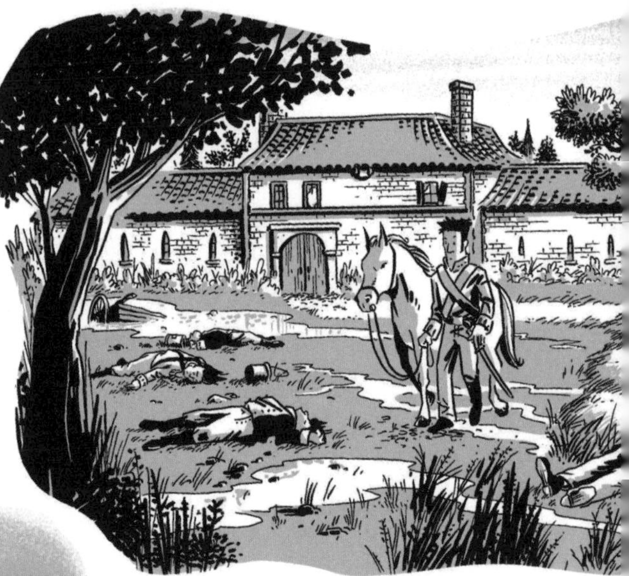

Napoleon Bonaparte's favorite horse, a grey Arabian stallion named Marengo, accompanied his master from his early battles through which Napoleon conquered most of Europe to his eventual defeat at Waterloo. Injured there, the horse was abandoned on the battlefield and taken by an enemy officer. He lived out his days in Britain, an object of curiosity and fascination.

Staff Sergeant Reckless was purchased from a stableboy in Seoul by US. Marines in the Korean War. Trained as a pack horse, Reckless carried supplies, evacuated the wounded, was himself wounded in battle, received the Purple Heart, and became a minor celebrity upon his return to the United States. Most famously, Reckless once made 51 consecutive resupply trips in a single day to and from the front lines during the Battle for Outpost Vegas.

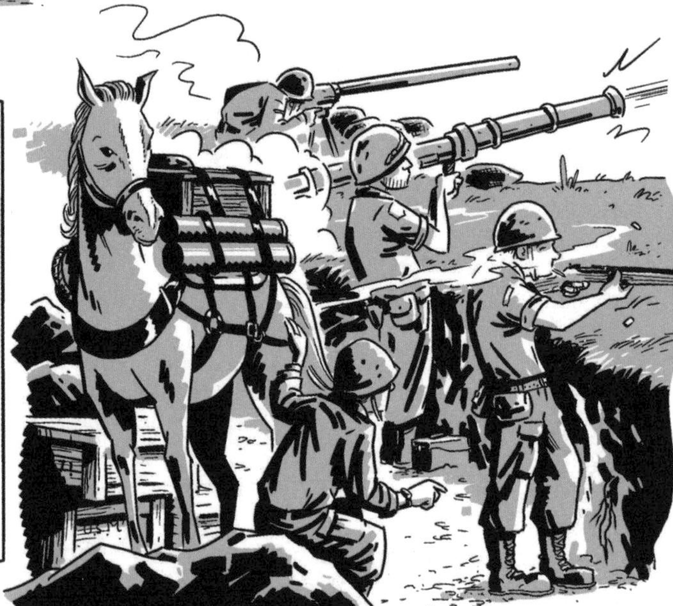

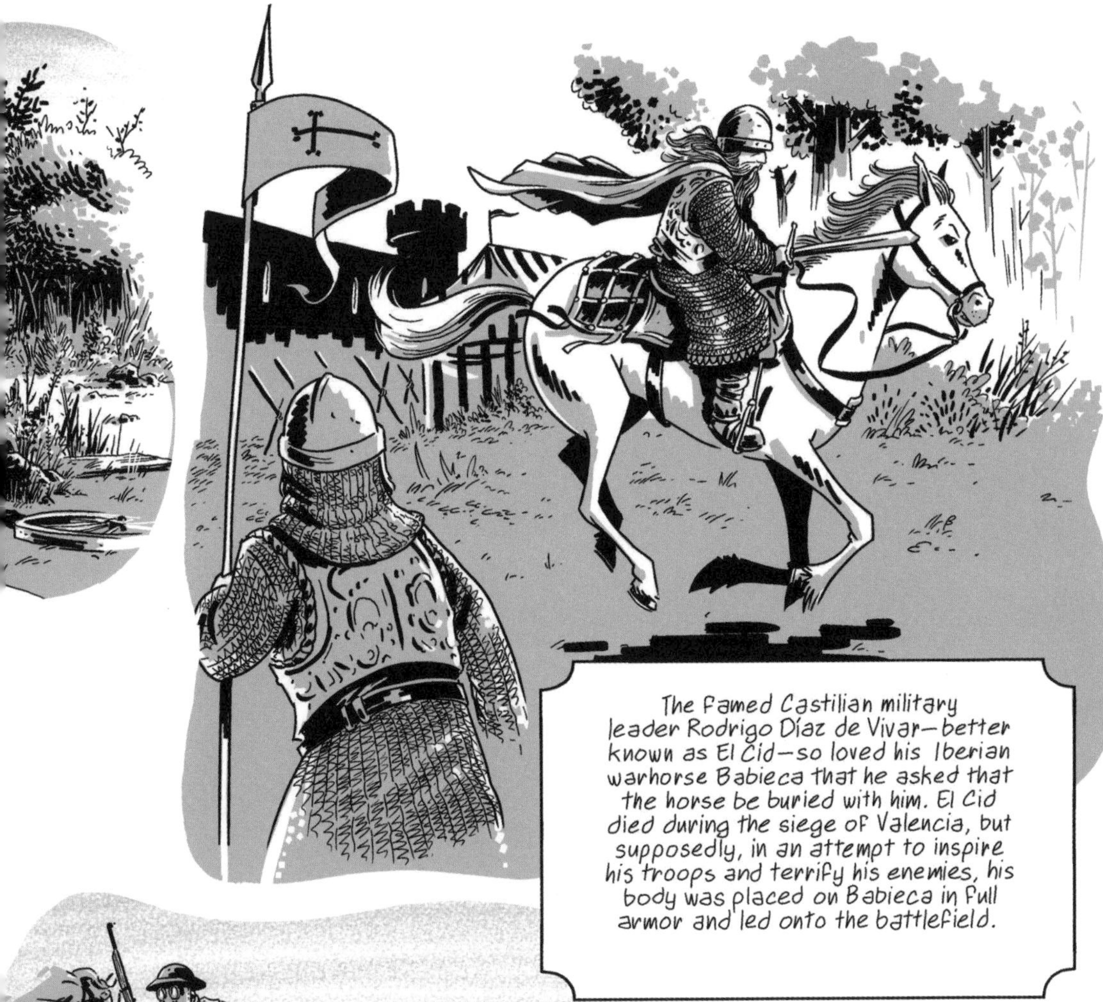
The famed Castilian military leader Rodrigo Díaz de Vivar—better known as El Cid—so loved his Iberian warhorse Babieca that he asked that the horse be buried with him. El Cid died during the siege of Valencia, but supposedly, in an attempt to inspire his troops and terrify his enemies, his body was placed on Babieca in full armor and led onto the battlefield.

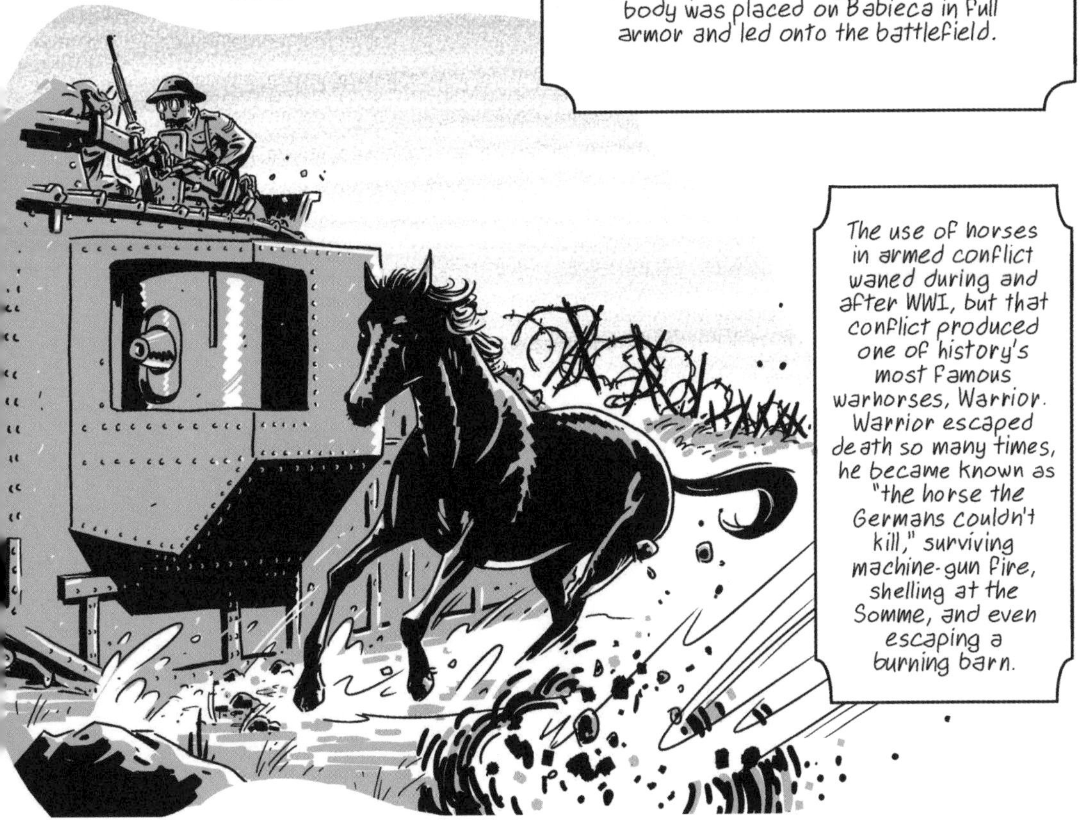
The use of horses in armed conflict waned during and after WWI, but that conflict produced one of history's most famous warhorses, Warrior. Warrior escaped death so many times, he became known as "the horse the Germans couldn't kill," surviving machine-gun fire, shelling at the Somme, and even escaping a burning barn.

CARRIER
PIGEONS

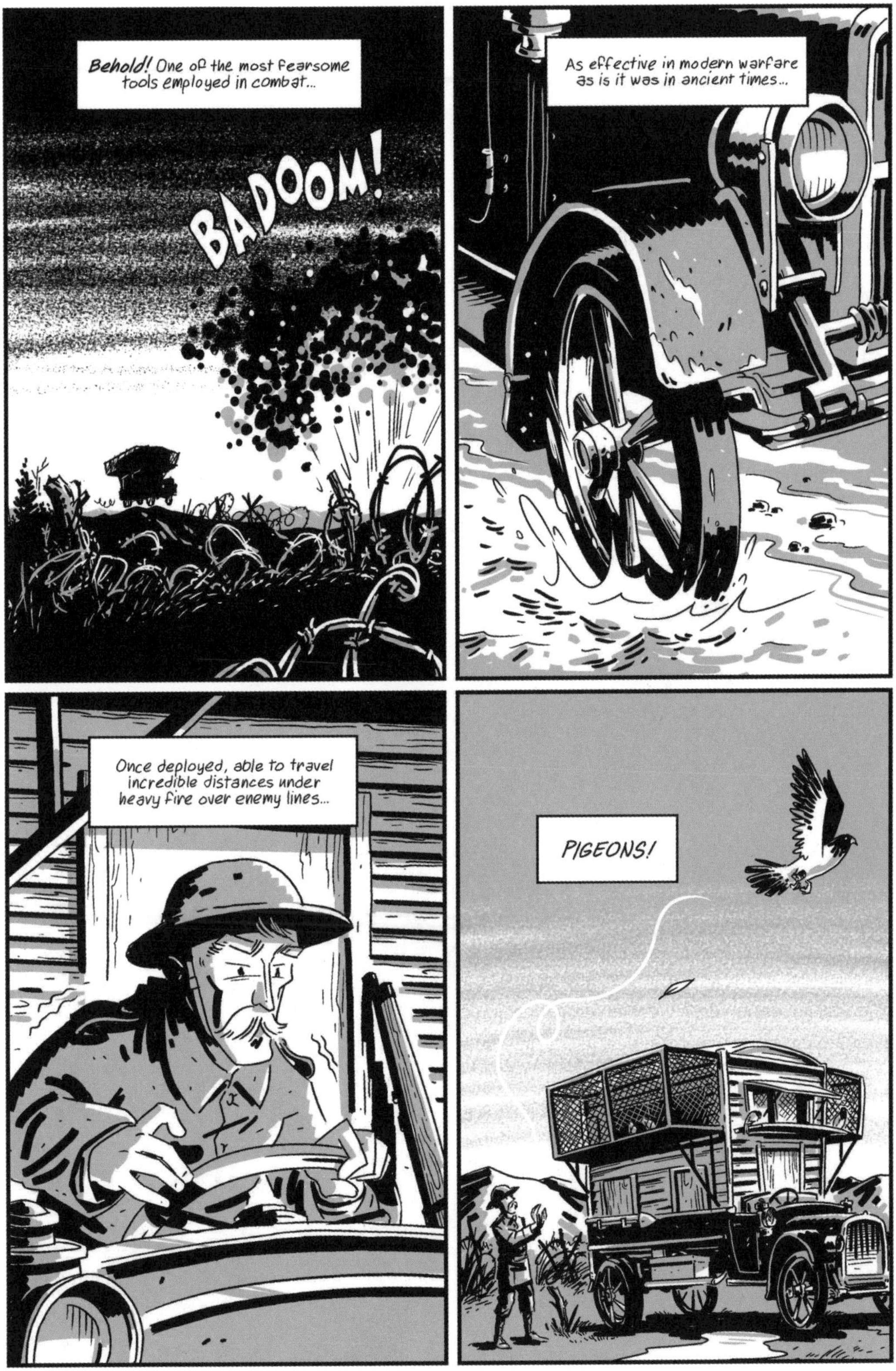

Behold! One of the most fearsome tools employed in combat...
BADOOM!
As effective in modern warfare as is it was in ancient times...
Once deployed, able to travel incredible distances under heavy fire over enemy lines...
PIGEONS!

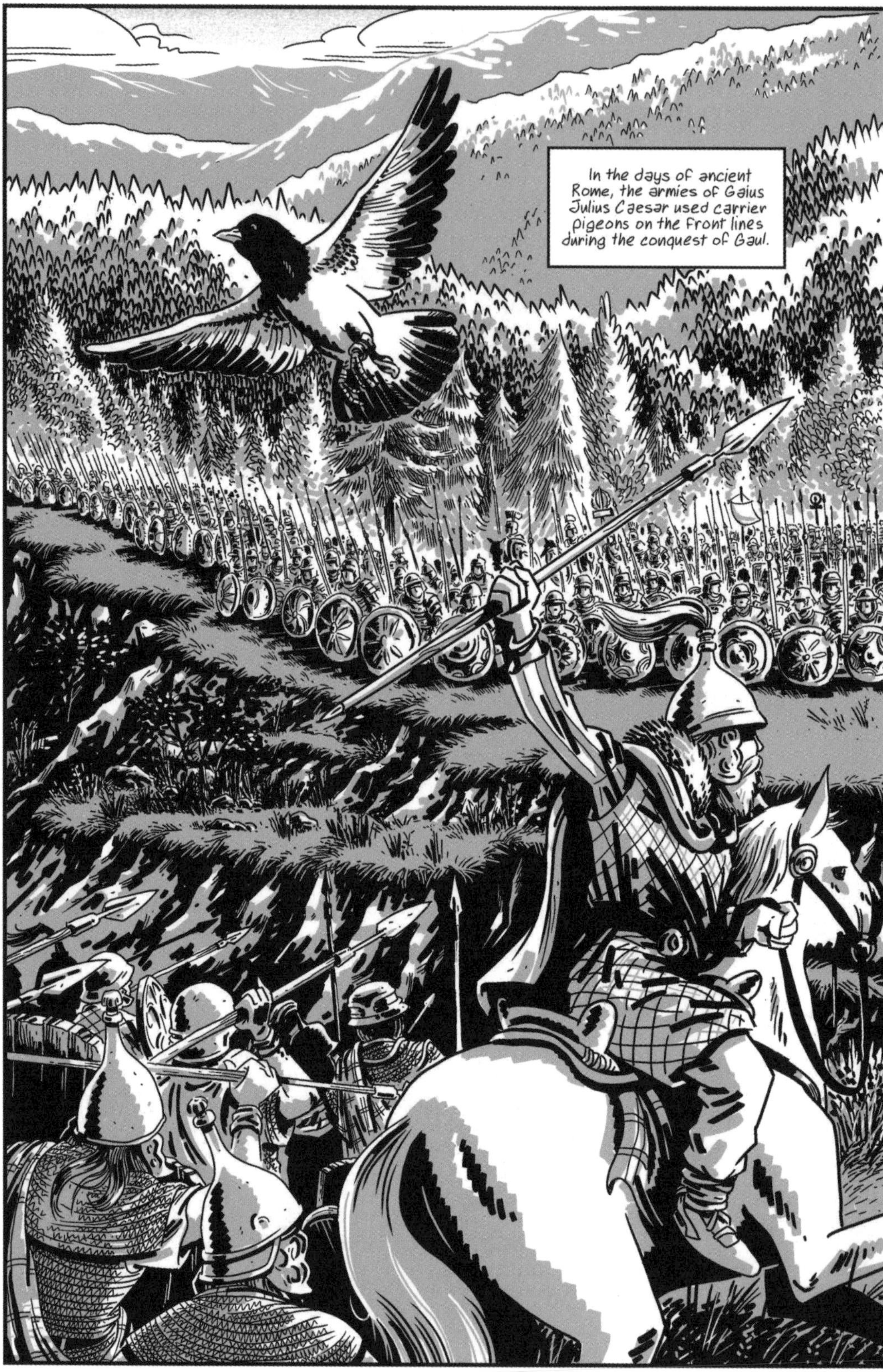
In the days of ancient Rome, the armies of Gaius Julius Caesar used carrier pigeons on the front lines during the conquest of Gaul.

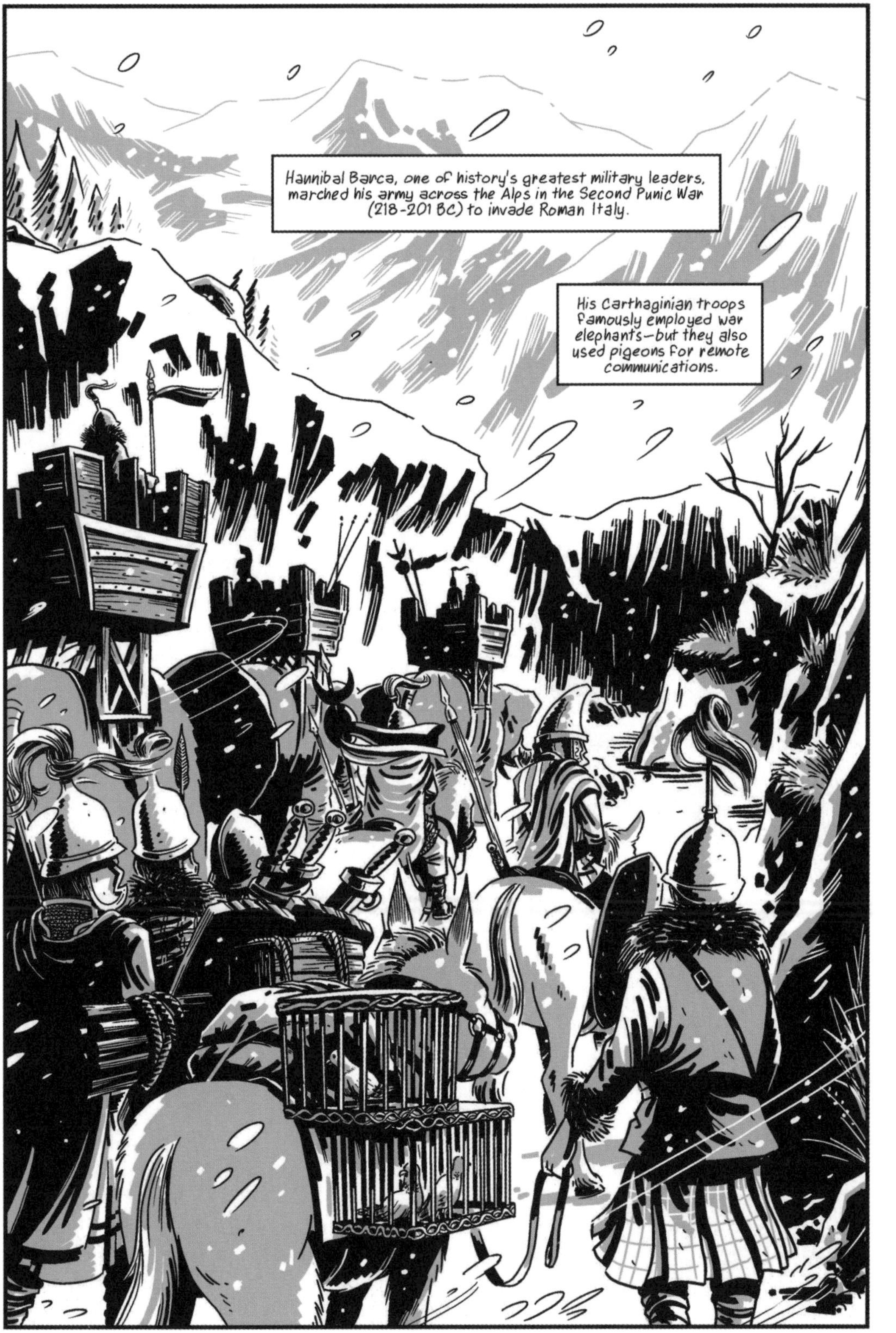
Hannibal Barca, one of history's greatest military leaders, marched his army across the Alps in the Second Punic War (218-201 BC) to invade Roman Italy.
His Carthaginian troops famously employed war elephants—but they also used pigeons for remote communications.

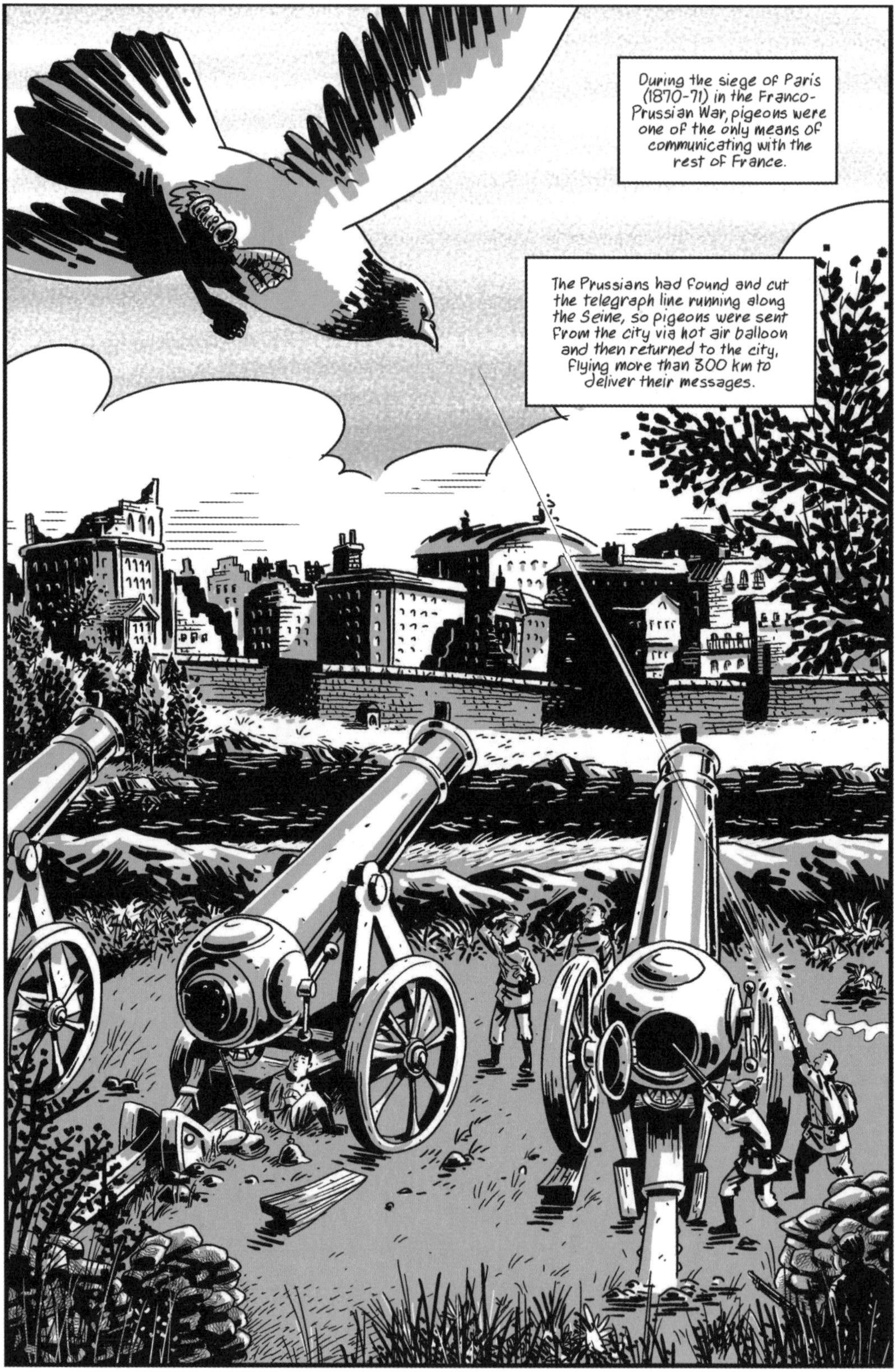
During the siege of Paris (1870-71) in the Franco-Prussian War, pigeons were one of the only means of communicating with the rest of France.
The Prussians had found and cut the telegraph line running along the Seine, so pigeons were sent from the city via hot air balloon and then returned to the city, flying more than 300 km to deliver their messages.

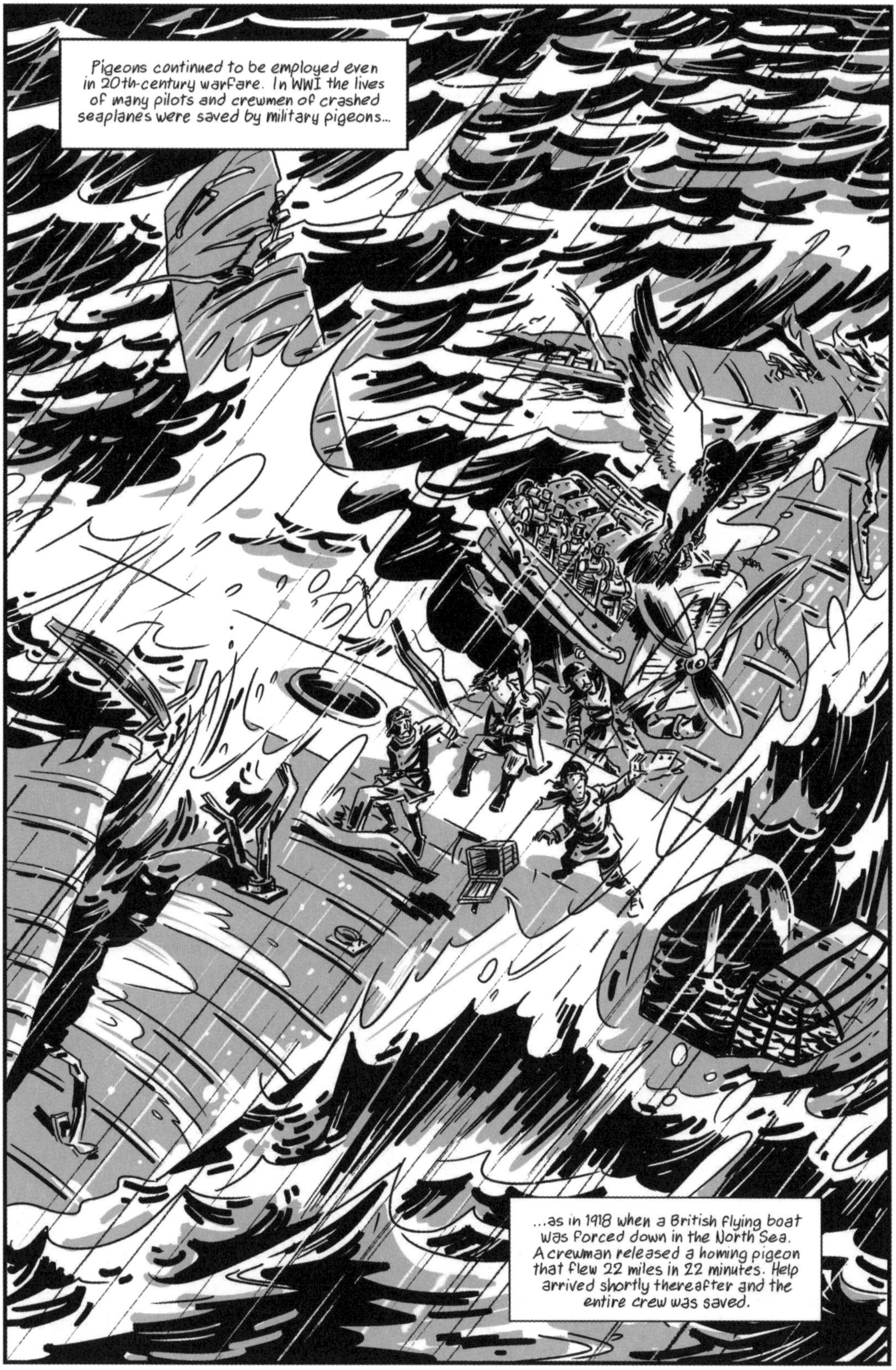
Pigeons continued to be employed even in 20th-century warfare. In WWI the lives of many pilots and crewmen of crashed seaplanes were saved by military pigeons...
...as in 1918 when a British flying boat was forced down in the North Sea. A crewman released a homing pigeon that flew 22 miles in 22 minutes. Help arrived shortly thereafter and the entire crew was saved.

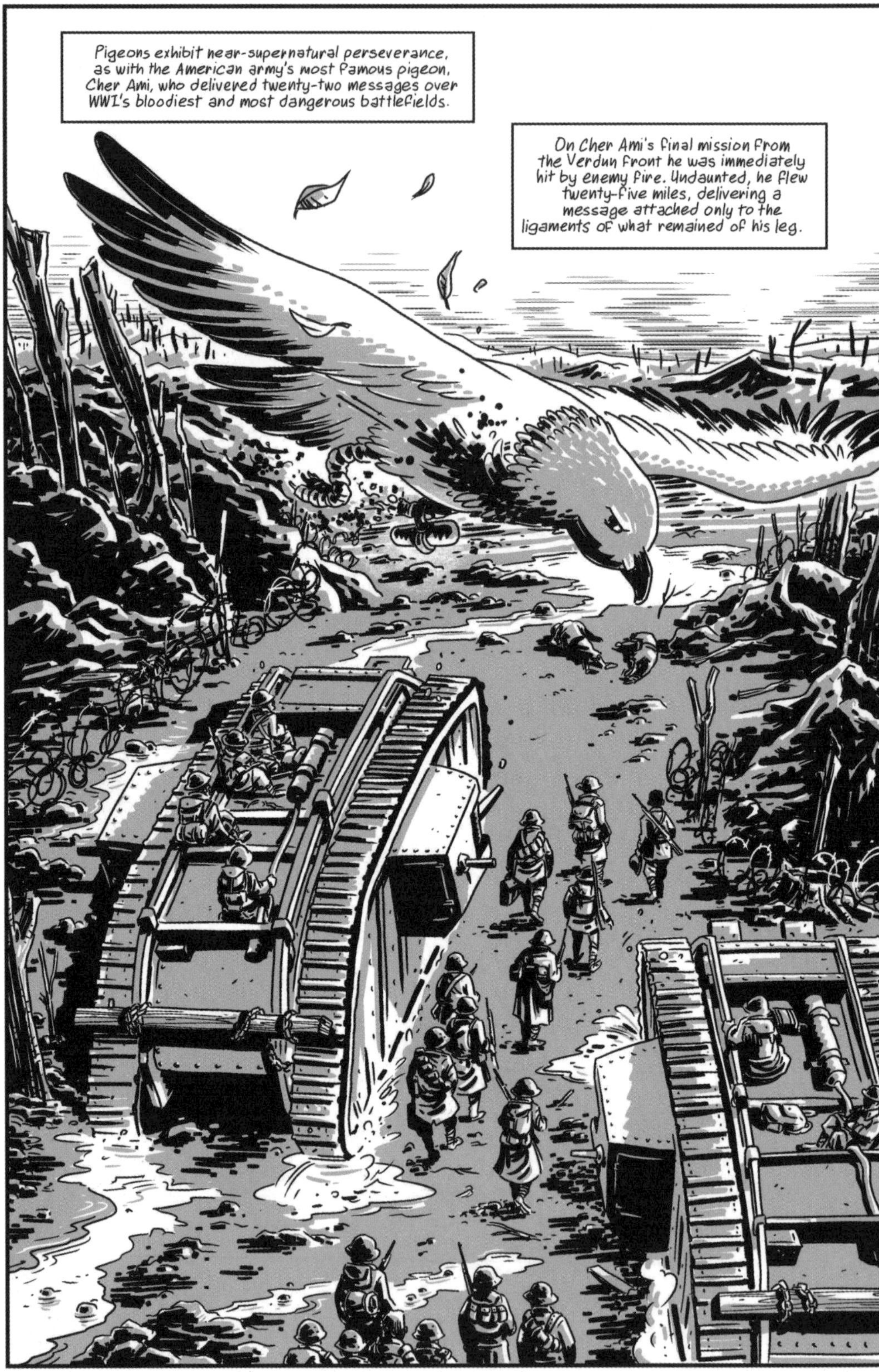
Pigeons exhibit near-supernatural perseverance, as with the American army's most famous pigeon, Cher Ami, who delivered twenty-two messages over WWI's bloodiest and most dangerous battlefields.
On Cher Ami's final mission from the Verdun front he was immediately hit by enemy fire. Undaunted, he flew twenty-five miles, delivering a message attached only to the ligaments of what remained of his leg.

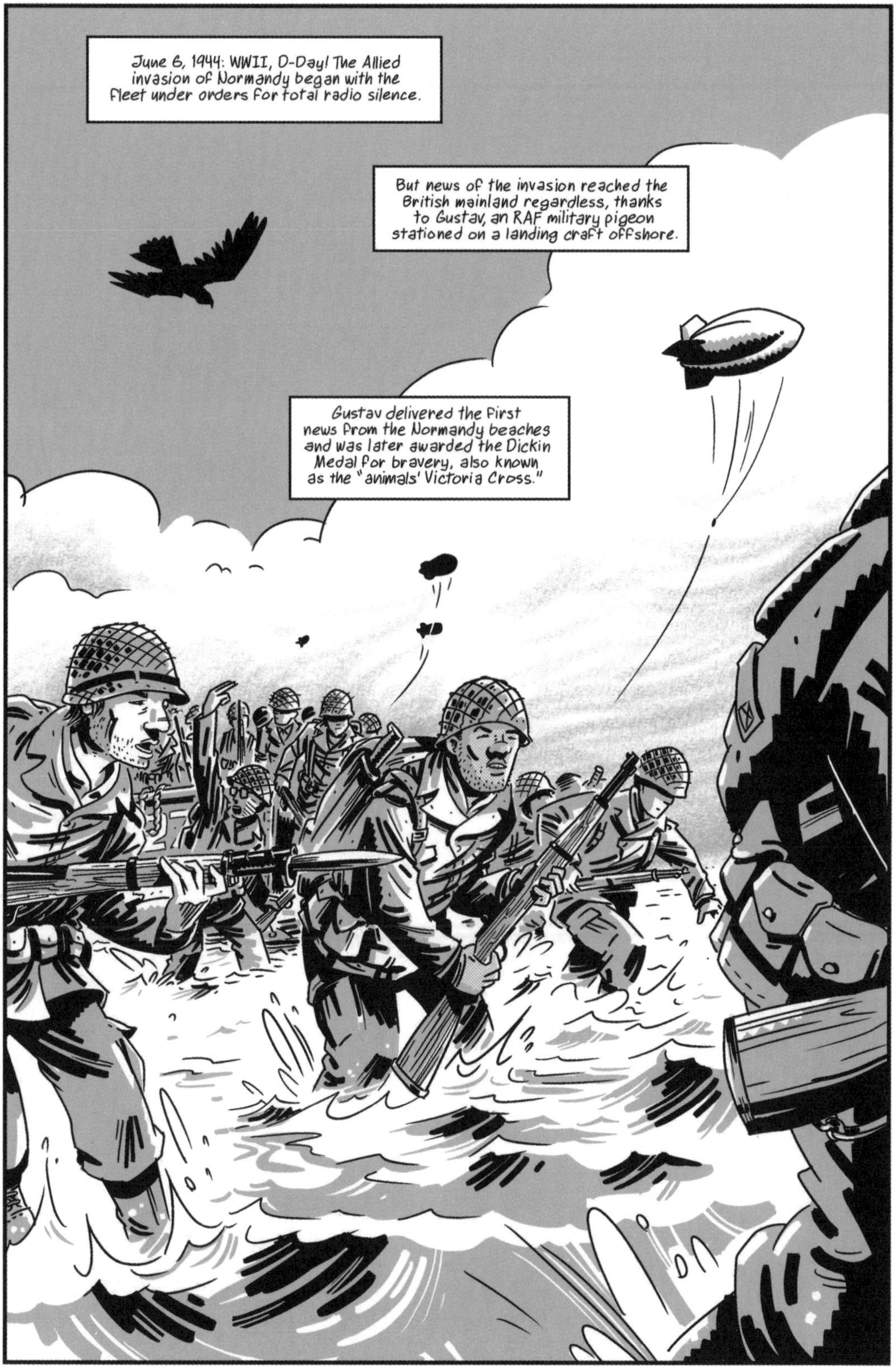
June 6, 1944: WWII, D-Day! The Allied invasion of Normandy began with the fleet under orders for total radio silence.
But news of the invasion reached the British mainland regardless, thanks to Gustav, an RAF military pigeon stationed on a landing craft offshore.
Gustav delivered the first news from the Normandy beaches and was later awarded the Dickin Medal for bravery, also known as the "animals' Victoria Cross."

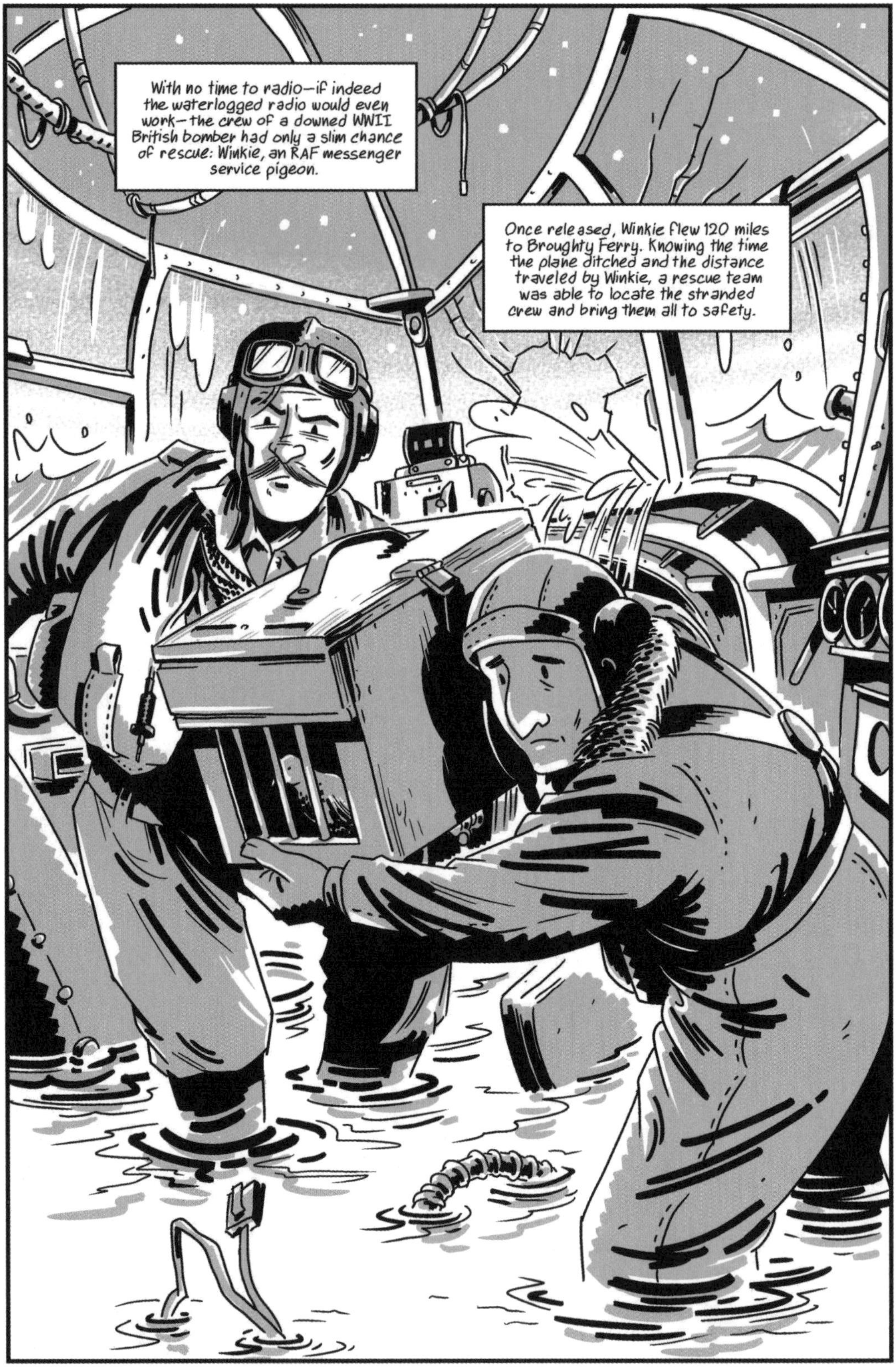
With no time to radio—if indeed the waterlogged radio would even work—the crew of a downed WWII British bomber had only a slim chance of rescue: Winkie, an RAF messenger service pigeon.
Once released, Winkie flew 120 miles to Broughty Ferry. Knowing the time the plane ditched and the distance traveled by Winkie, a rescue team was able to locate the stranded crew and bring them all to safety.

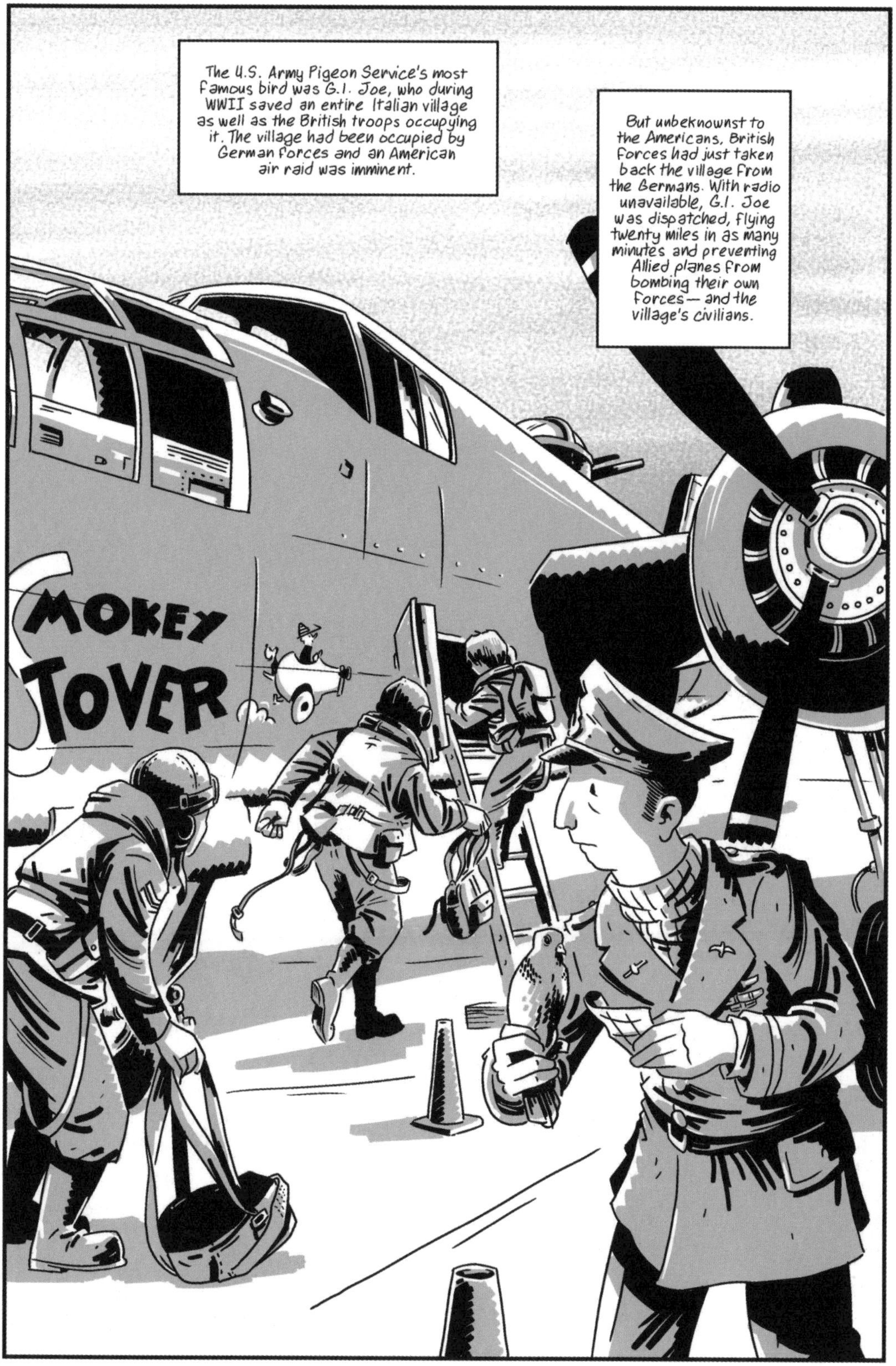
The U.S. Army Pigeon Service's most famous bird was G.I. Joe, who during WWII saved an entire Italian village as well as the British troops occupying it. The village had been occupied by German forces and an American air raid was imminent.
But unbeknownst to the Americans, British forces had just taken back the village from the Germans. With radio unavailable, G.I. Joe was dispatched, flying twenty miles in as many minutes and preventing Allied planes from bombing their own forces— and the village's civilians.
MOKEY
TOVER

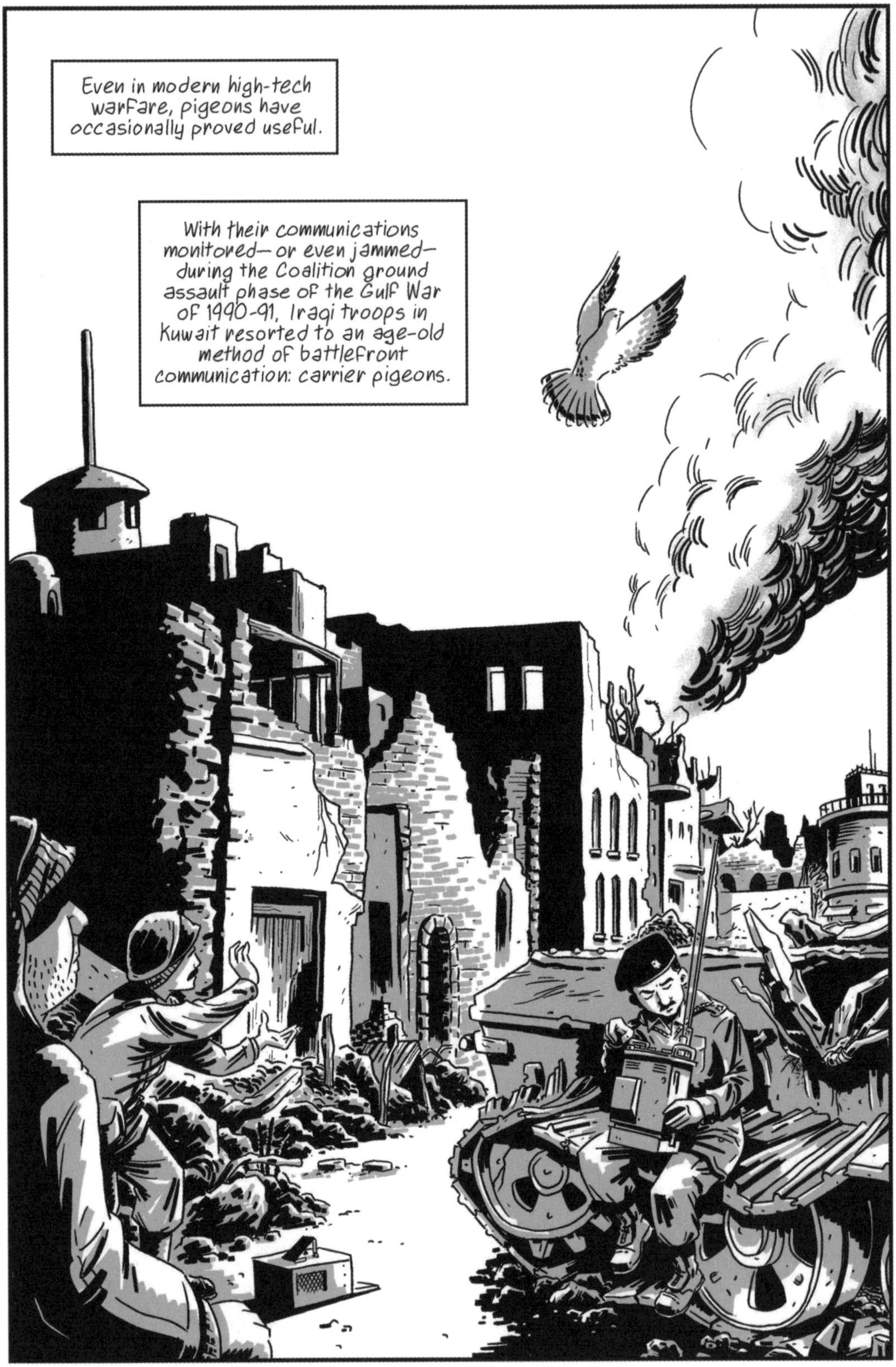
Even in modern high-tech warfare, pigeons have occasionally proved useful.
With their communications monitored—or even jammed—during the Coalition ground assault phase of the Gulf War of 1990-91, Iraqi troops in Kuwait resorted to an age-old method of battlefront communication: carrier pigeons.

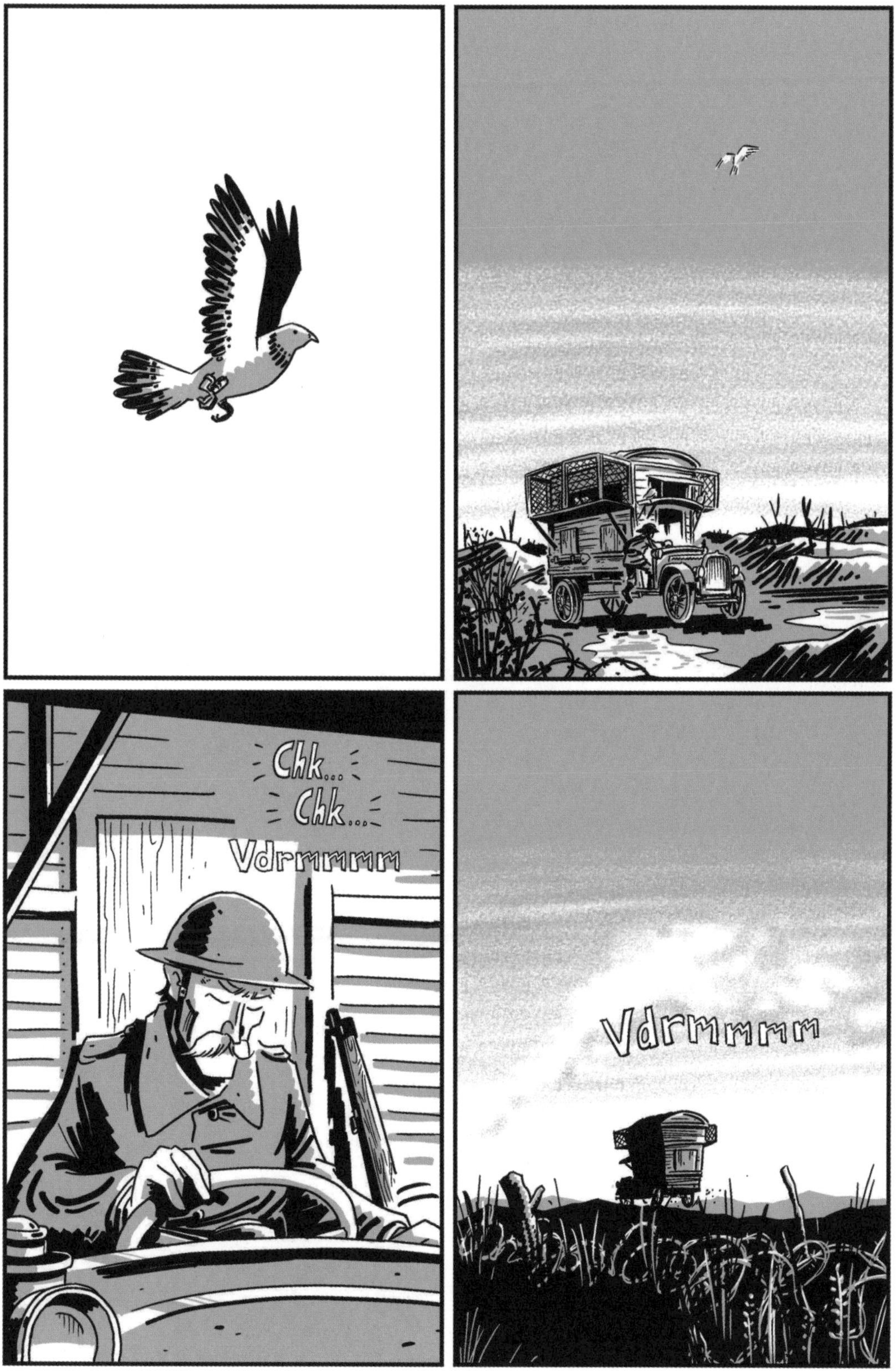
Chk...
Chk...
Vdrmmmm
Vdrmmmm

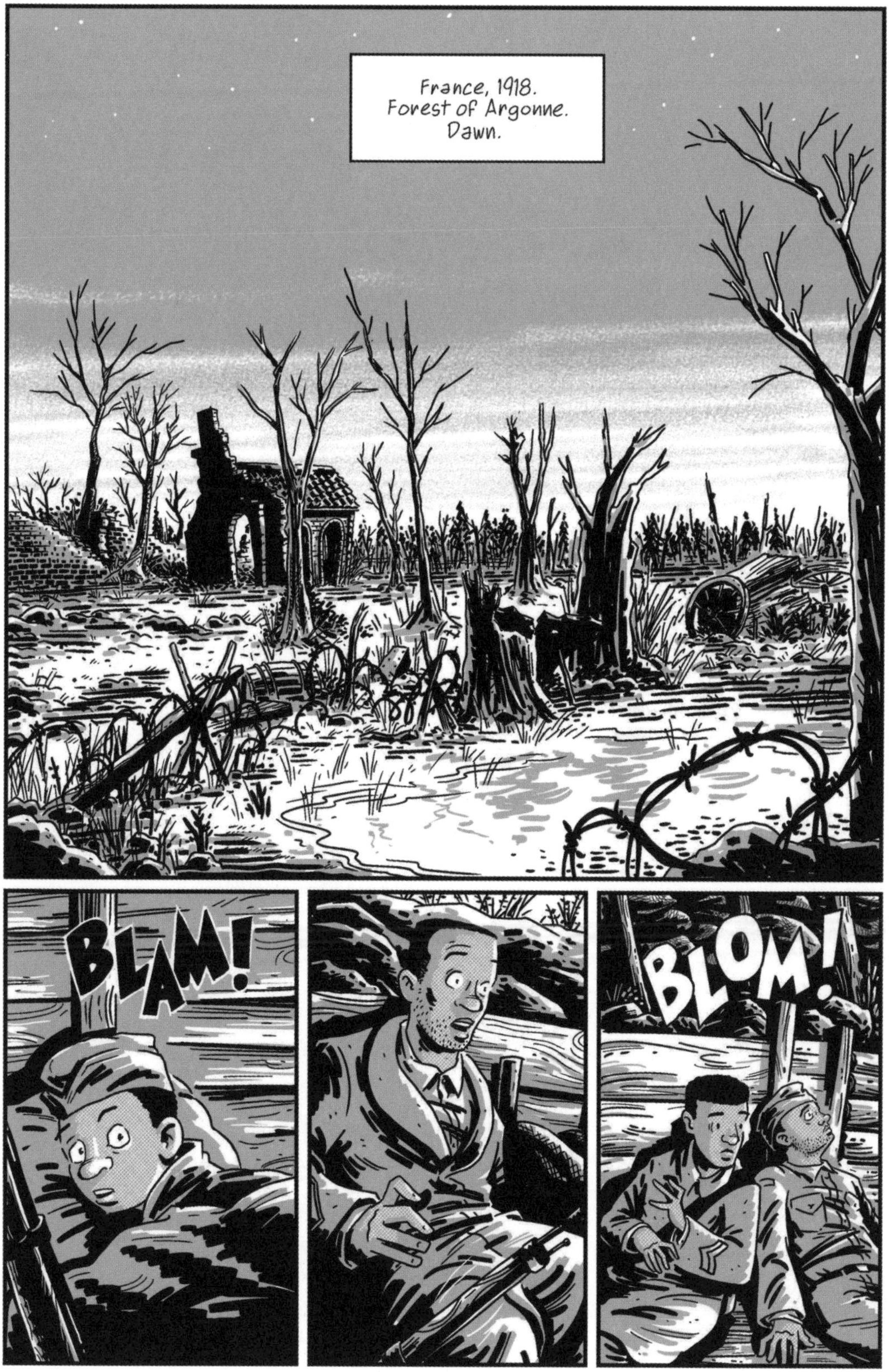
France, 1918.
Forest of Argonne.
Dawn.
BLAM!
BLOM!

BADOOM!

ABOUT THE
CREATOR

BEN TOWLE is a four-time Eisner-nominated cartoonist.
His previous work, the rollicking nautical fantasy comic
Oyster War, was published by Oni Press in 2015. His
other work includes *Amelia Earhart: This Broad Ocean*
(with Sarah Stewart Taylor), a graphic novel for young
adults (Disney/Hyperion Books, 2010) that received
accolades from such publications as the *New York Times*
and *Publishers Weekly* and was a Junior Library Guild
selection, as well as the historical fiction graphic novel
Midnight Sun and a volume of comics folk tales, *Farewell,
Georgia*. He lives in Columbus, Ohio, and is a professor
of illustration at the Columbus College of Art and Design.